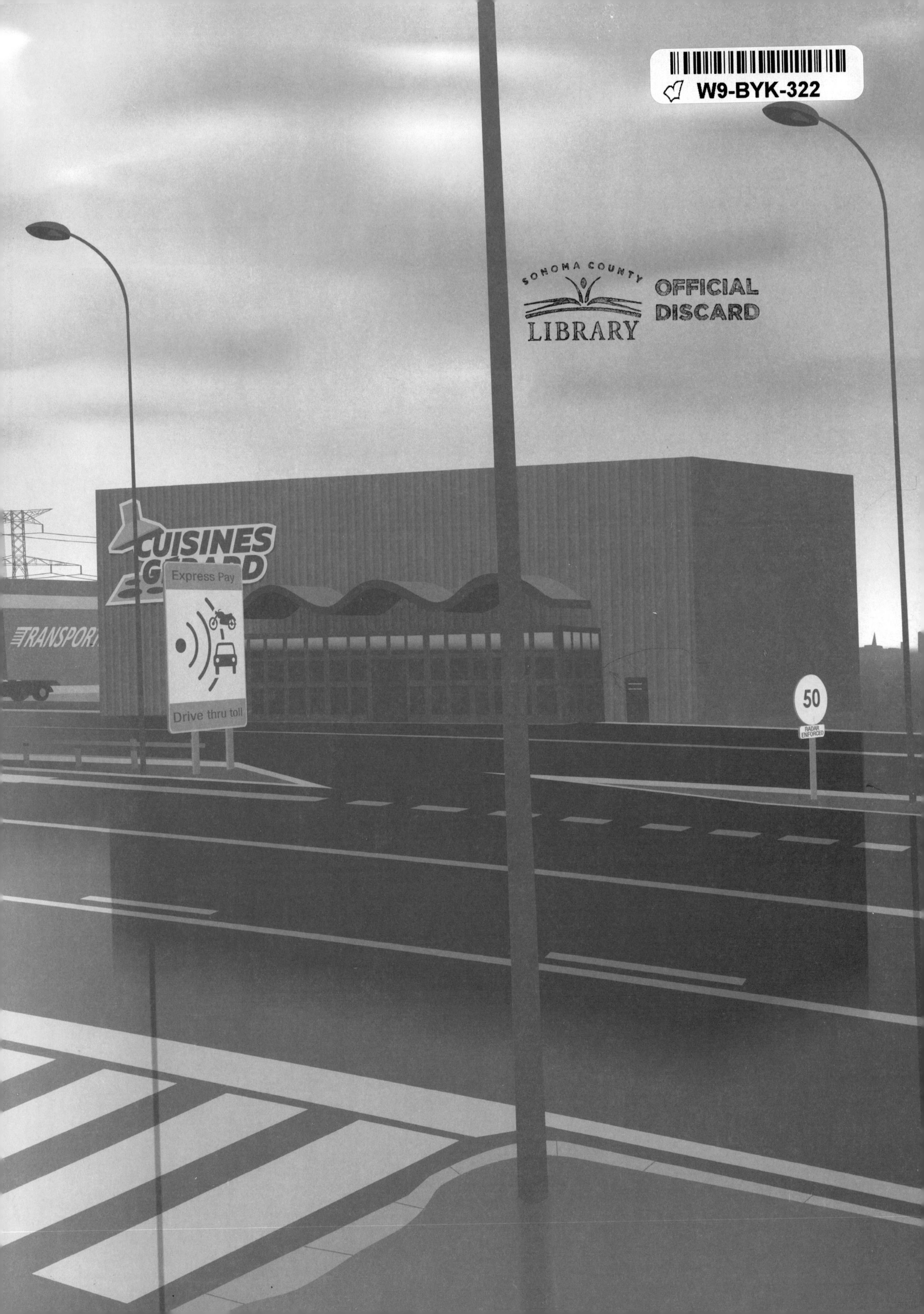
CUISINES
Express Pay
Drive thru toll
TRANSPORT
50
RADAR ENFORCED

All pages of this story (except the cover) were (again)
created in Adobe Illustrator 9.0.

Thanks to the whole team at Dupuis, as well as to the
readers of Spirou for their messages of encouragement
all along the episodic serialization of this story.

Any resemblance between the Gretchen character and
Aurelie C. is unintended only to the extent that
Gretchen prefers sushi to pizza.

ARTHUR DE PINS

www.zombillenium.com

ISBN 978-1-56163-850-5
© DUPUIS 2011, by De Pins
www.dupuis.com
All rights reserved.
© NBM, 2014 for the English translation
Library of Congress Control Number: 2013936651

Printed in China

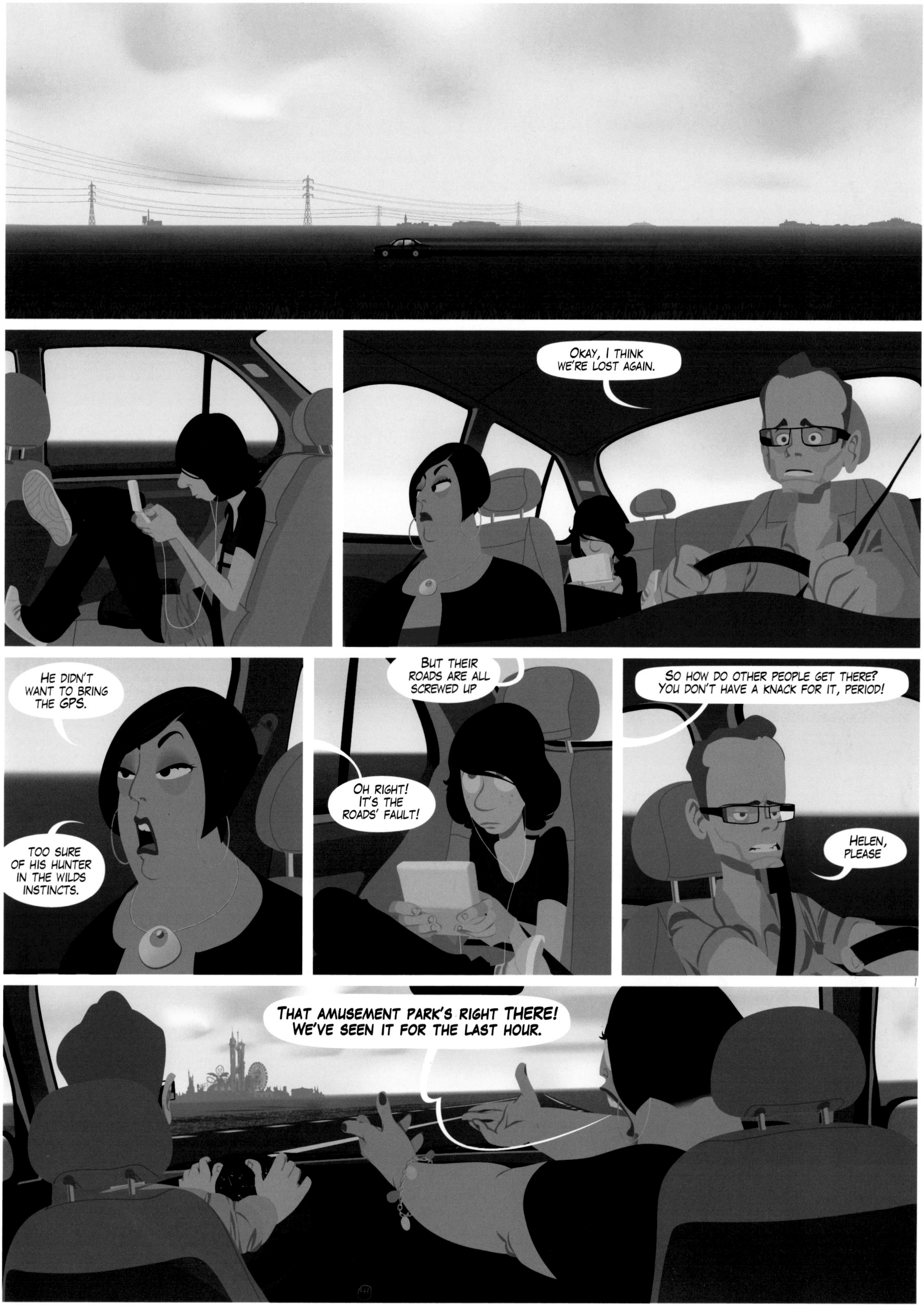
Okay, I think we're lost again.
He didn't want to bring the GPS.
Too sure of his hunter in the wilds instincts.
But their roads are all screwed up
Oh right! It's the roads' fault!
So how do other people get there? You don't have a knack for it, period!
Helen, please
That amusement park's right THERE! We've seen it for the last hour.

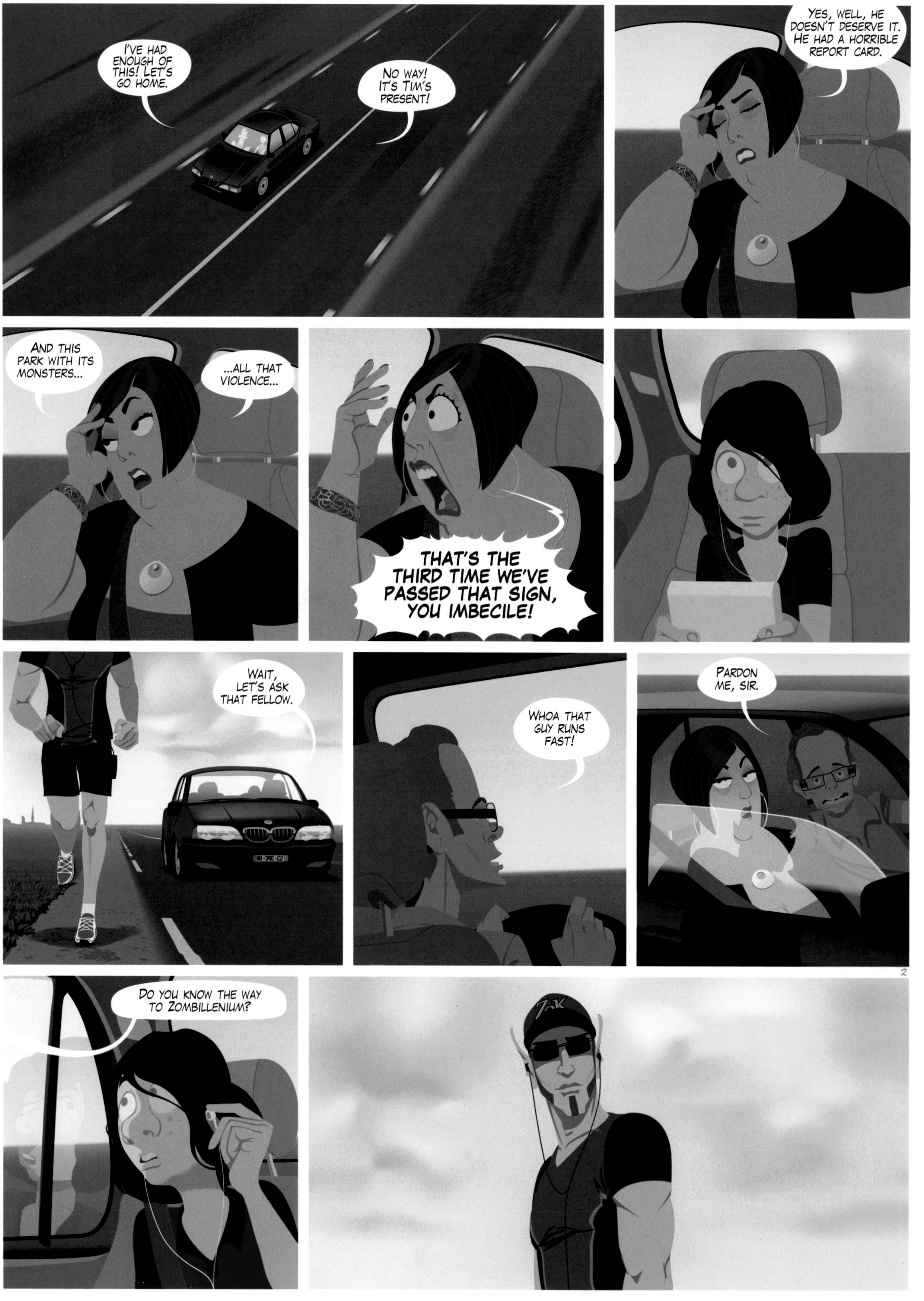
I'VE HAD ENOUGH OF THIS! LET'S GO HOME.
NO WAY! IT'S TIM'S PRESENT!
YES, WELL, HE DOESN'T DESERVE IT. HE HAD A HORRIBLE REPORT CARD.
AND THIS PARK WITH ITS MONSTERS...
...ALL THAT VIOLENCE...
THAT'S THE THIRD TIME WE'VE PASSED THAT SIGN, YOU IMBECILE!
WAIT, LET'S ASK THAT FELLOW.
WHOA THAT GUY RUNS FAST!
PARDON ME, SIR.
DO YOU KNOW THE WAY TO ZOMBILLENIUM?

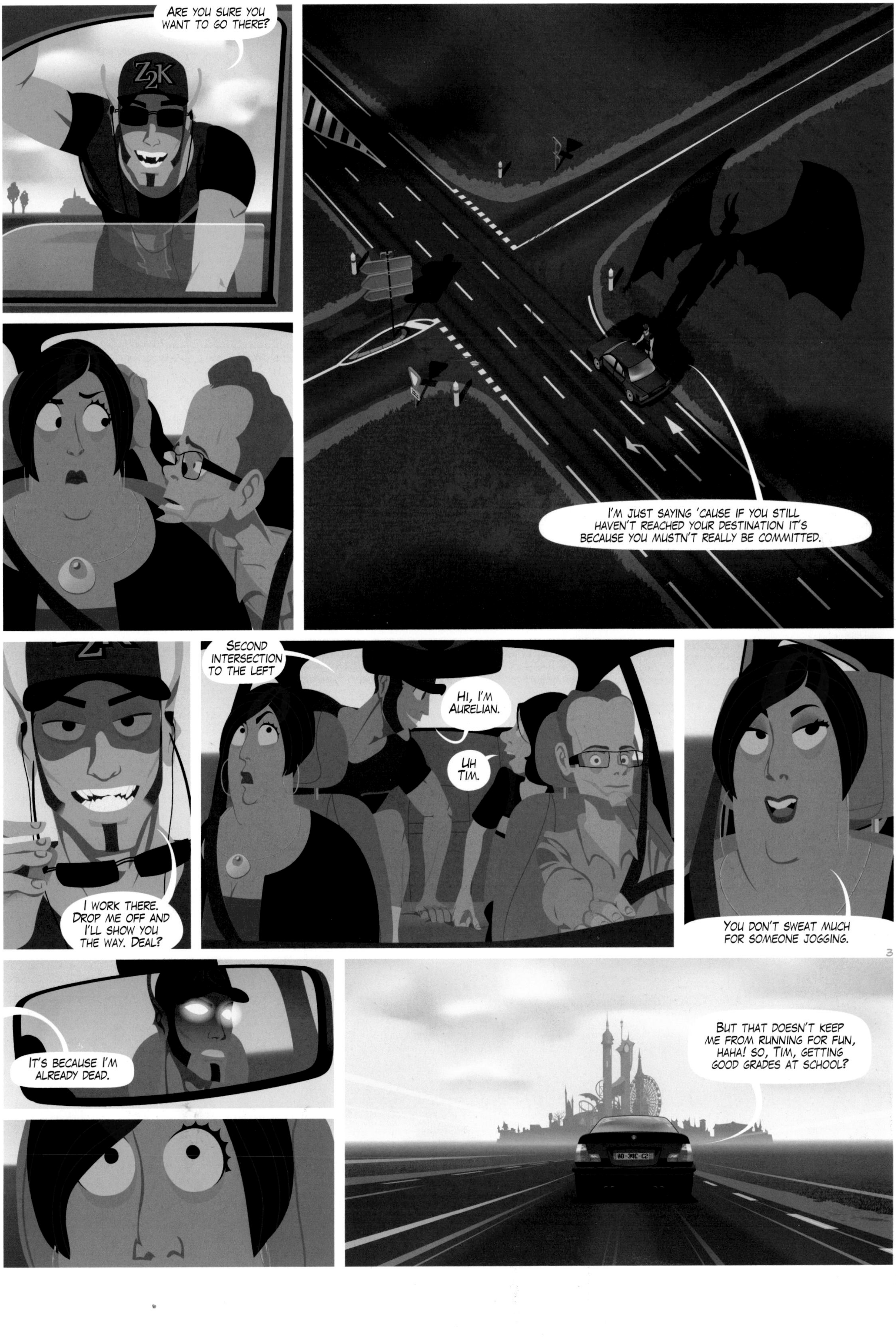
Are you sure you want to go there?
I'm just saying 'cause if you still haven't reached your destination it's because you mustn't really be committed.
I work there. Drop me off and I'll show you the way. Deal?
Second intersection to the left
Hi, I'm Aurelian.
Uh Tim.
You don't sweat much for someone jogging.
It's because I'm already dead.
But that doesn't keep me from running for fun, haha! So, Tim, getting good grades at school?

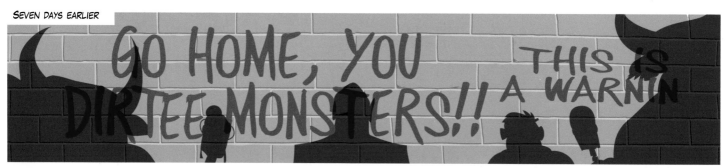

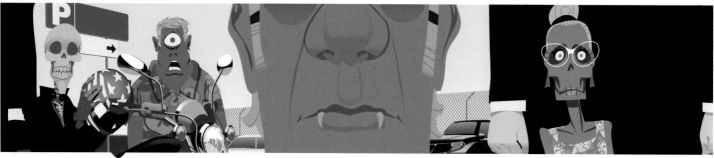

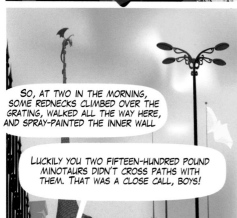

SEVEN DAYS EARLIER
GO HOME, YOU DIRTEE MONSTERS!!
THIS IS A WARNIN
SO, AT TWO IN THE MORNING, SOME REDNECKS CLIMBED OVER THE GRATING, WALKED ALL THE WAY HERE, AND SPRAY-PAINTED THE INNER WALL
LUCKILY YOU TWO FIFTEEN-HUNDRED POUND MINOTAURS DIDN'T CROSS PATHS WITH THEM. THAT WAS A CLOSE CALL, BOYS!
WE'RE SORRY, MR. VON BLOODT.
WE'D NODDED OFF.
WE'LL ERASE IT.
HEY, FRANCIS! MAYBE IT'S BEEN SIGNED BY THE DEVIL HIMSELF. IT LOOKS LIKE HIS WRITING.
YES, HE'S GIVING US VACATION.
TSSS YOU MORONS.
MISTER VON BLOODT?
THE MEETING WITH THE PARK RESTAURANT MANAGERS IS AT TWO.
OKAY.
THE TOYMAKER IS REQUESTING THE GO-AHEAD ON THE FIGURINES OF AURELIAN.
GRANTED.
SHOULD I RESERVE THE TEAM-BUILDING SEMINAR IN THE CARPATHIANS?
YES.
I HAVE SOME QUOTES ON THE ROLLERCOASTER MAINTENANCE.
TAKE THE LEAST EXPENSIVE.
THE GOLEMS ARE ASKING TO NOT WORK ON SATURDAYS.
SLURP!
FLAP
FLAP
FLAP
DENIED. JUST LIKE FOR SUNDAYS.
OTHERWISE, THE YOUNG INTERN...
GRETCHEN.
YES. SHE'S ASKING FOR TIME OFF TO GO SEE HER MOM IN ENGLAND.
GRANTED.
AH, AND UH ...

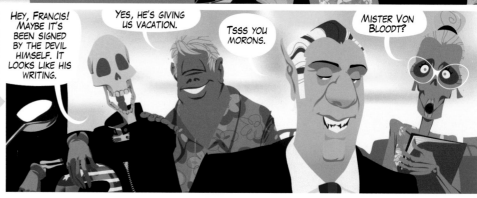

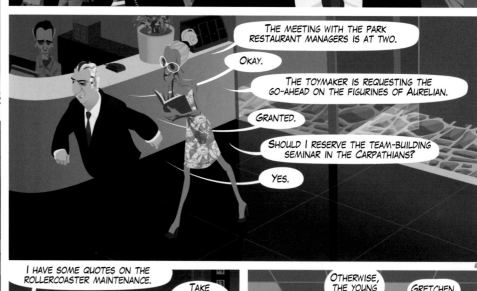

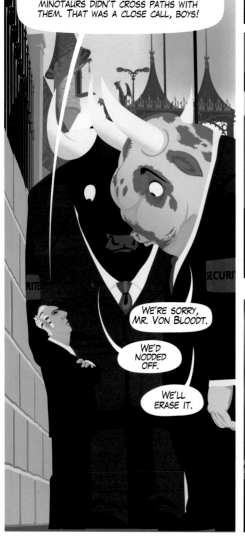

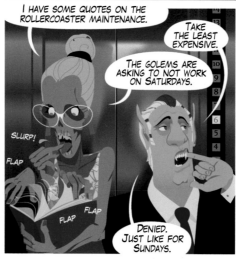

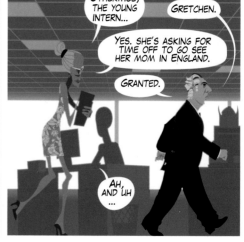

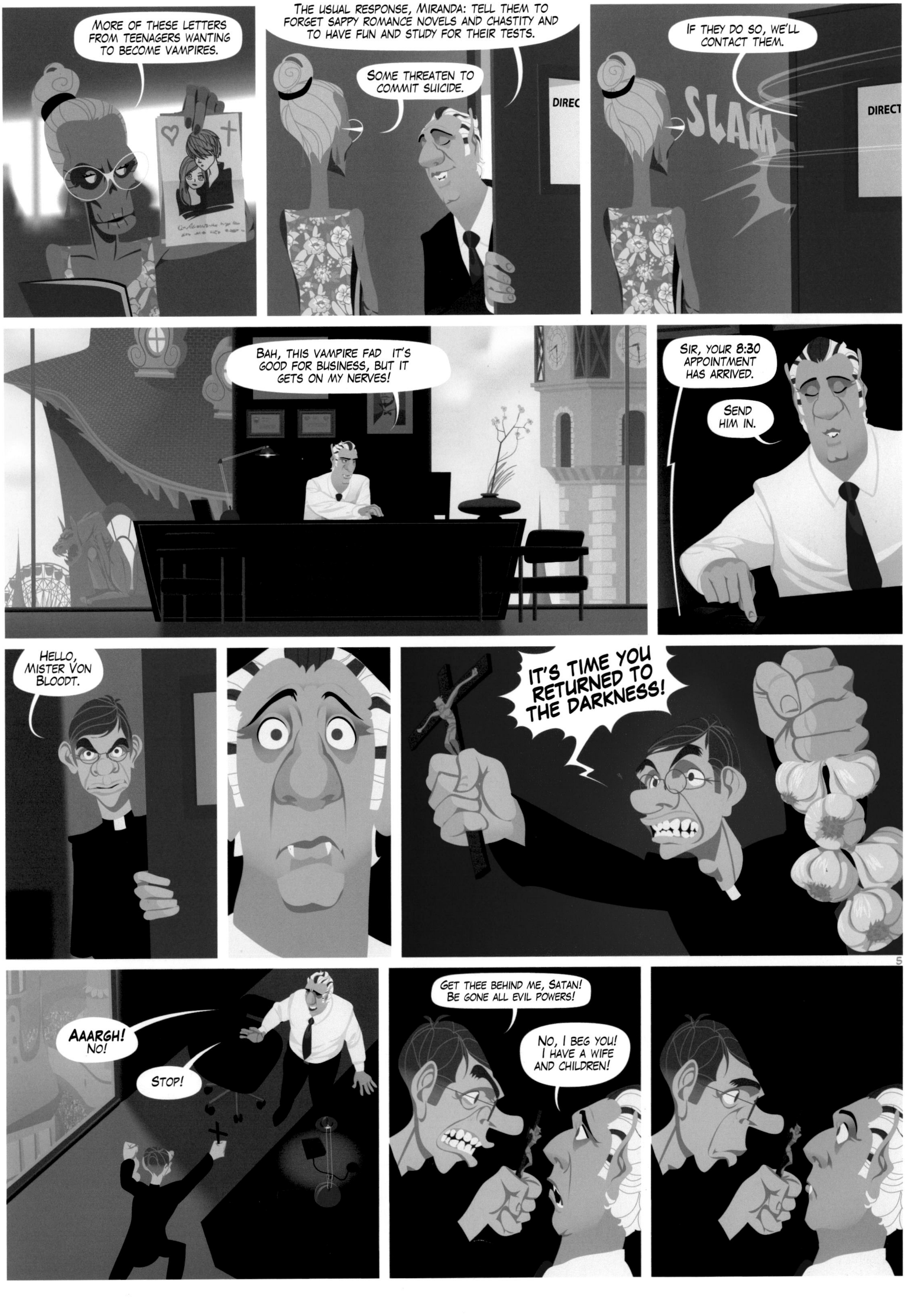
More of these letters from teenagers wanting to become vampires.
The usual response, Miranda: tell them to forget sappy romance novels and chastity and to have fun and study for their tests.
Some threaten to commit suicide.
DIREC
If they do so, we'll contact them.
SLAM
DIRECT
Bah, this vampire fad it's good for business, but it gets on my nerves!
Sir, your 8:30 appointment has arrived.
Send him in.
Hello, Mister Von Bloodt.
It's time you returned to the darkness!
AAARGH! No!
Stop!
Get thee behind me, Satan! Be gone all evil powers!
No, I beg you! I have a wife and children!

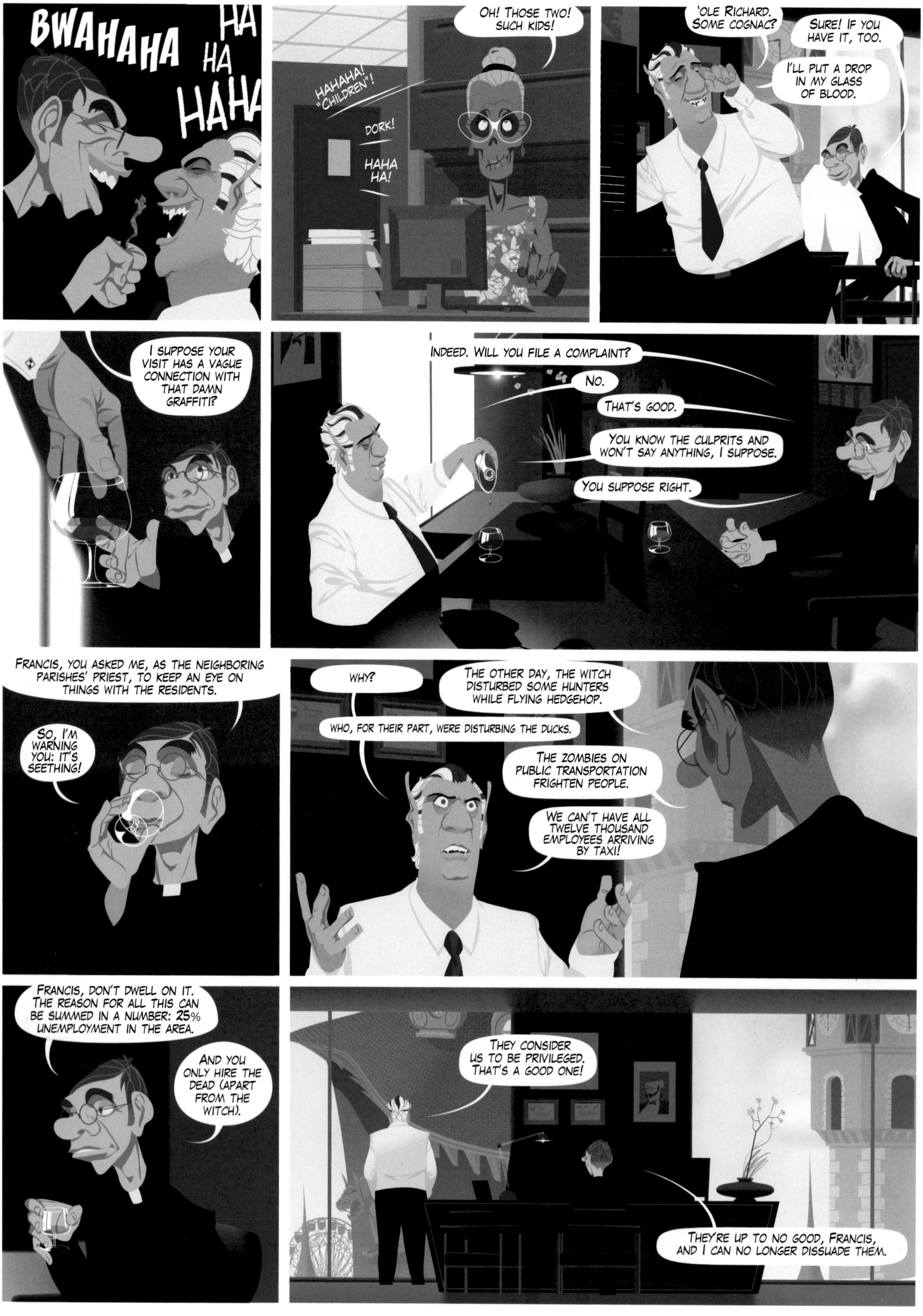
BWAHAHA
HA HA HAHA
OH! THOSE TWO! SUCH KIDS!
HAHAHA! "CHILDREN"!
DORK!
HAHA HA!
'OLE RICHARD. SOME COGNAC?
SURE! IF YOU HAVE IT, TOO.
I'LL PUT A DROP IN MY GLASS OF BLOOD.
I SUPPOSE YOUR VISIT HAS A VAGUE CONNECTION WITH THAT DAMN GRAFFITI?
INDEED. WILL YOU FILE A COMPLAINT?
NO.
THAT'S GOOD.
YOU KNOW THE CULPRITS AND WON'T SAY ANYTHING, I SUPPOSE.
YOU SUPPOSE RIGHT.
FRANCIS, YOU ASKED ME, AS THE NEIGHBORING PARISHES' PRIEST, TO KEEP AN EYE ON THINGS WITH THE RESIDENTS.
SO, I'M WARNING YOU: IT'S SEETHING!
WHY?
THE OTHER DAY, THE WITCH DISTURBED SOME HUNTERS WHILE FLYING HEDGEHOP.
WHO, FOR THEIR PART, WERE DISTURBING THE DUCKS.
THE ZOMBIES ON PUBLIC TRANSPORTATION FRIGHTEN PEOPLE.
WE CAN'T HAVE ALL TWELVE THOUSAND EMPLOYEES ARRIVING BY TAXI!
FRANCIS, DON'T DWELL ON IT. THE REASON FOR ALL THIS CAN BE SUMMED IN A NUMBER: 25% UNEMPLOYMENT IN THE AREA.
AND YOU ONLY HIRE THE DEAD (APART FROM THE WITCH).
THEY CONSIDER US TO BE PRIVILEGED. THAT'S A GOOD ONE!
THEY'RE UP TO NO GOOD, FRANCIS, AND I CAN NO LONGER DISSUADE THEM.

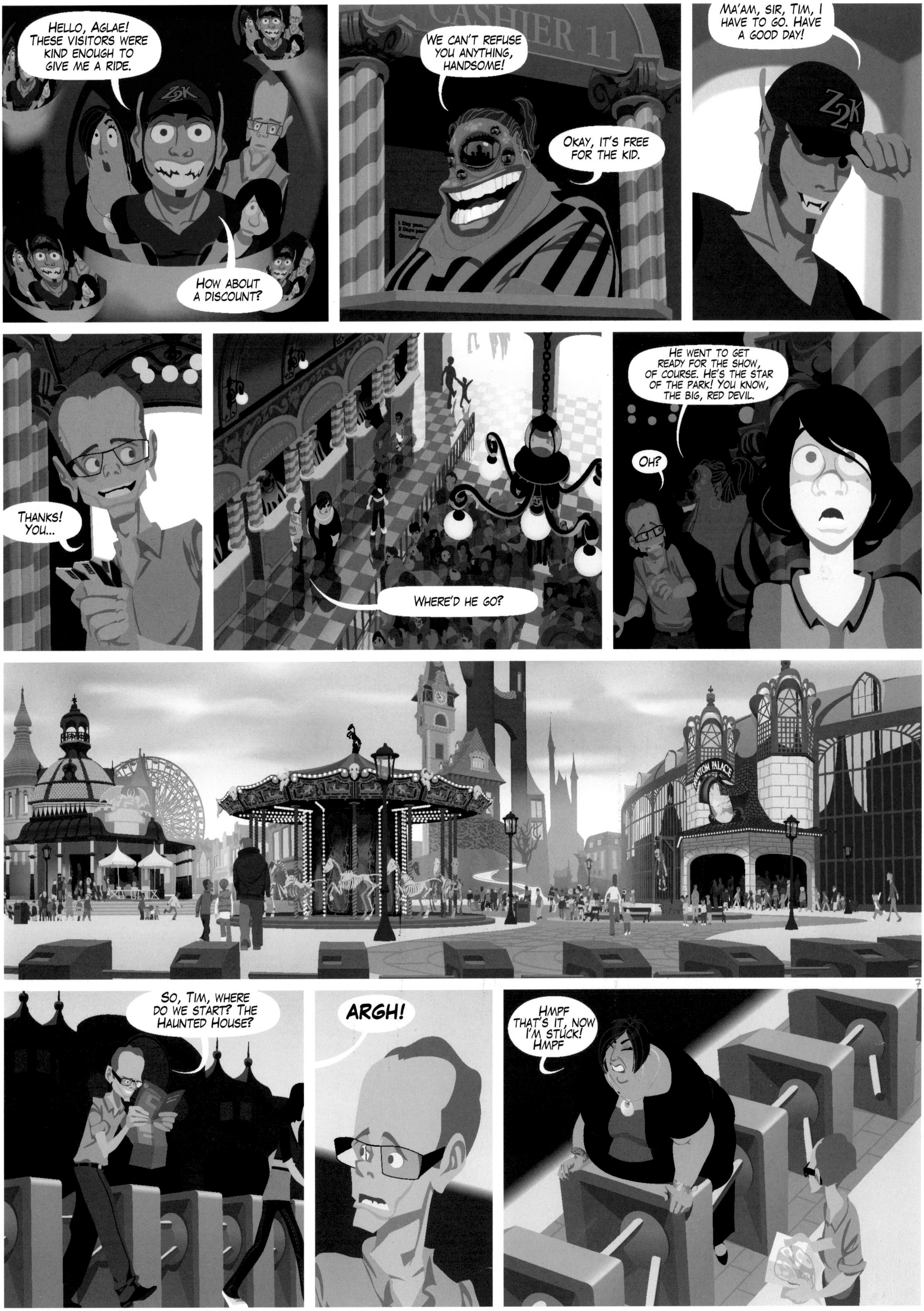

HELLO, AGLAE! THESE VISITORS WERE KIND ENOUGH TO GIVE ME A RIDE.
HOW ABOUT A DISCOUNT?
CASHIER 11
WE CAN'T REFUSE YOU ANYTHING, HANDSOME!
OKAY, IT'S FREE FOR THE KID.
MA'AM, SIR, TIM, I HAVE TO GO. HAVE A GOOD DAY!
THANKS! YOU...
WHERE'D HE GO?
HE WENT TO GET READY FOR THE SHOW, OF COURSE. HE'S THE STAR OF THE PARK! YOU KNOW, THE BIG, RED DEVIL.
OH?
PHANTOM PALACE
SO, TIM, WHERE DO WE START? THE HAUNTED HOUSE?
ARGH!
HMPF THAT'S IT, NOW I'M STUCK! HMPF

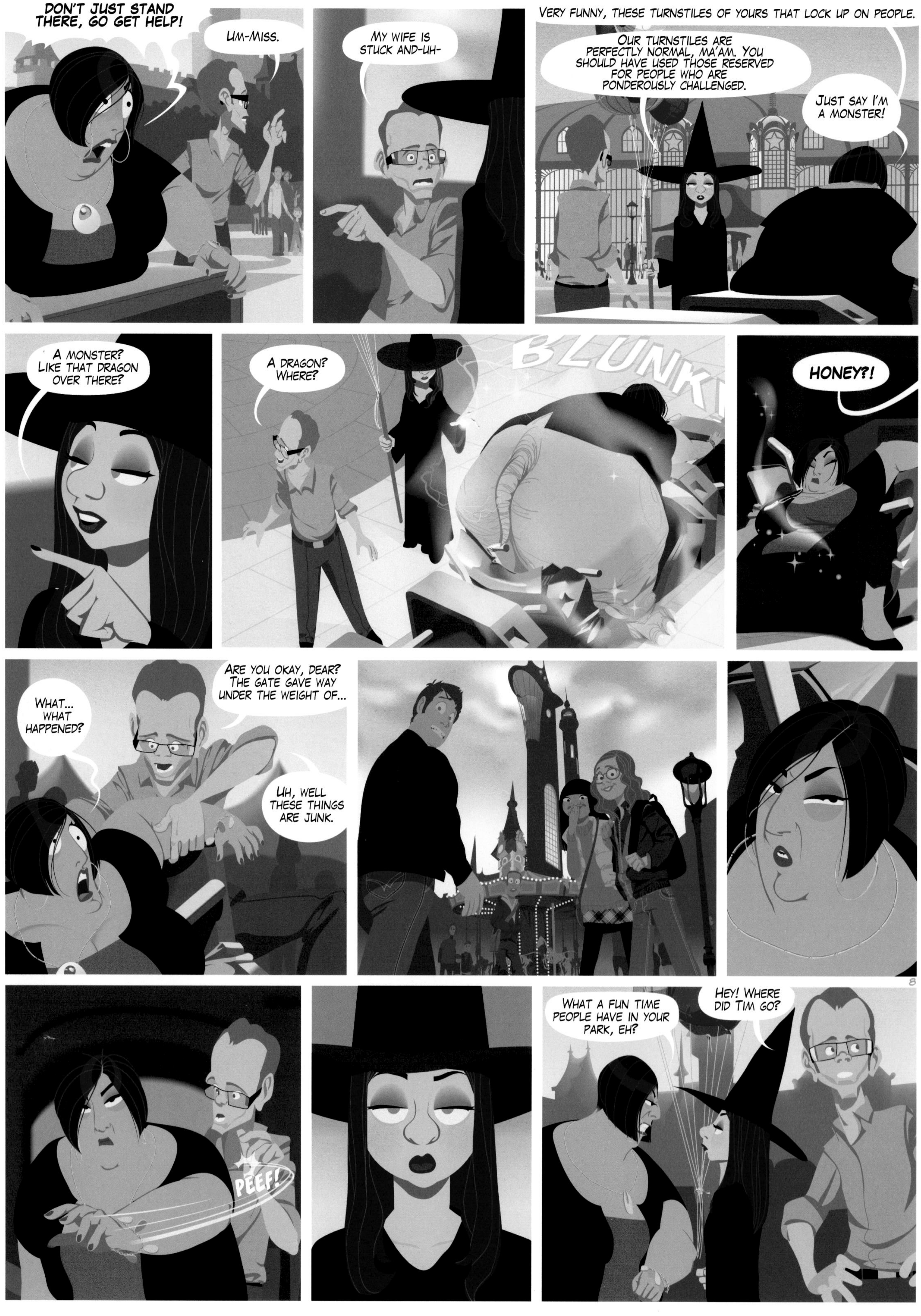
DON'T JUST STAND THERE, GO GET HELP!
UM-MISS.
MY WIFE IS STUCK AND-UH-
VERY FUNNY, THESE TURNSTILES OF YOURS THAT LOCK UP ON PEOPLE.
OUR TURNSTILES ARE PERFECTLY NORMAL, MA'AM. YOU SHOULD HAVE USED THOSE RESERVED FOR PEOPLE WHO ARE PONDEROUSLY CHALLENGED.
JUST SAY I'M A MONSTER!
A MONSTER? LIKE THAT DRAGON OVER THERE?
A DRAGON? WHERE?
BLUNK!
HONEY?!
WHAT... WHAT HAPPENED?
ARE YOU OKAY, DEAR? THE GATE GAVE WAY UNDER THE WEIGHT OF...
UH, WELL THESE THINGS ARE JUNK.
PEEF!
WHAT A FUN TIME PEOPLE HAVE IN YOUR PARK, EH?
HEY! WHERE DID TIM GO?

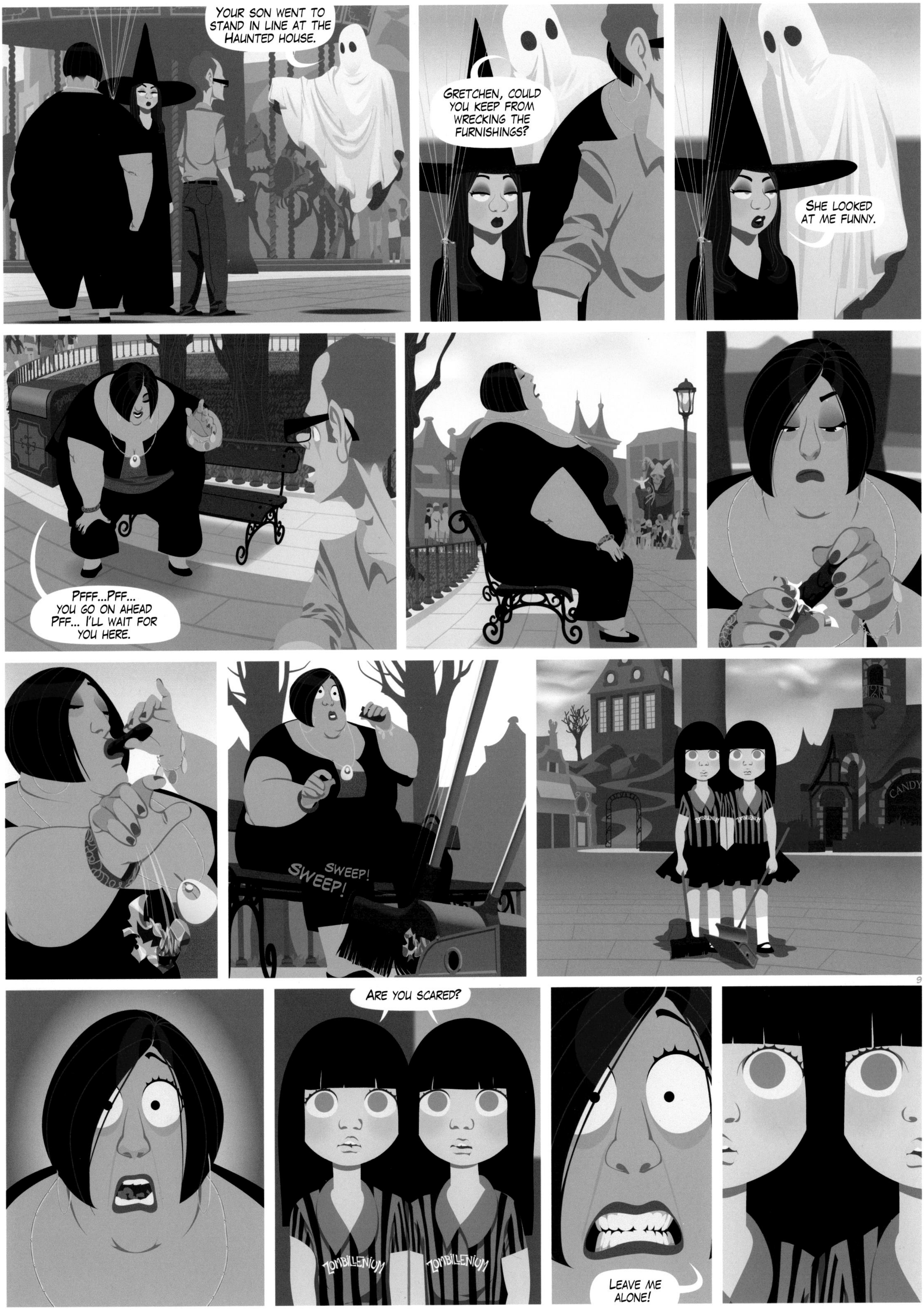
YOUR SON WENT TO STAND IN LINE AT THE HAUNTED HOUSE.
GRETCHEN, COULD YOU KEEP FROM WRECKING THE FURNISHINGS?
SHE LOOKED AT ME FUNNY.
PFFF...PFF... YOU GO ON AHEAD PFF... I'LL WAIT FOR YOU HERE.
SWEEP! SWEEP!
CANDY
ZOMBILLENIUM
ARE YOU SCARED?
ZOMBILLENIUM
ZOMBILLENIUM
LEAVE ME ALONE!

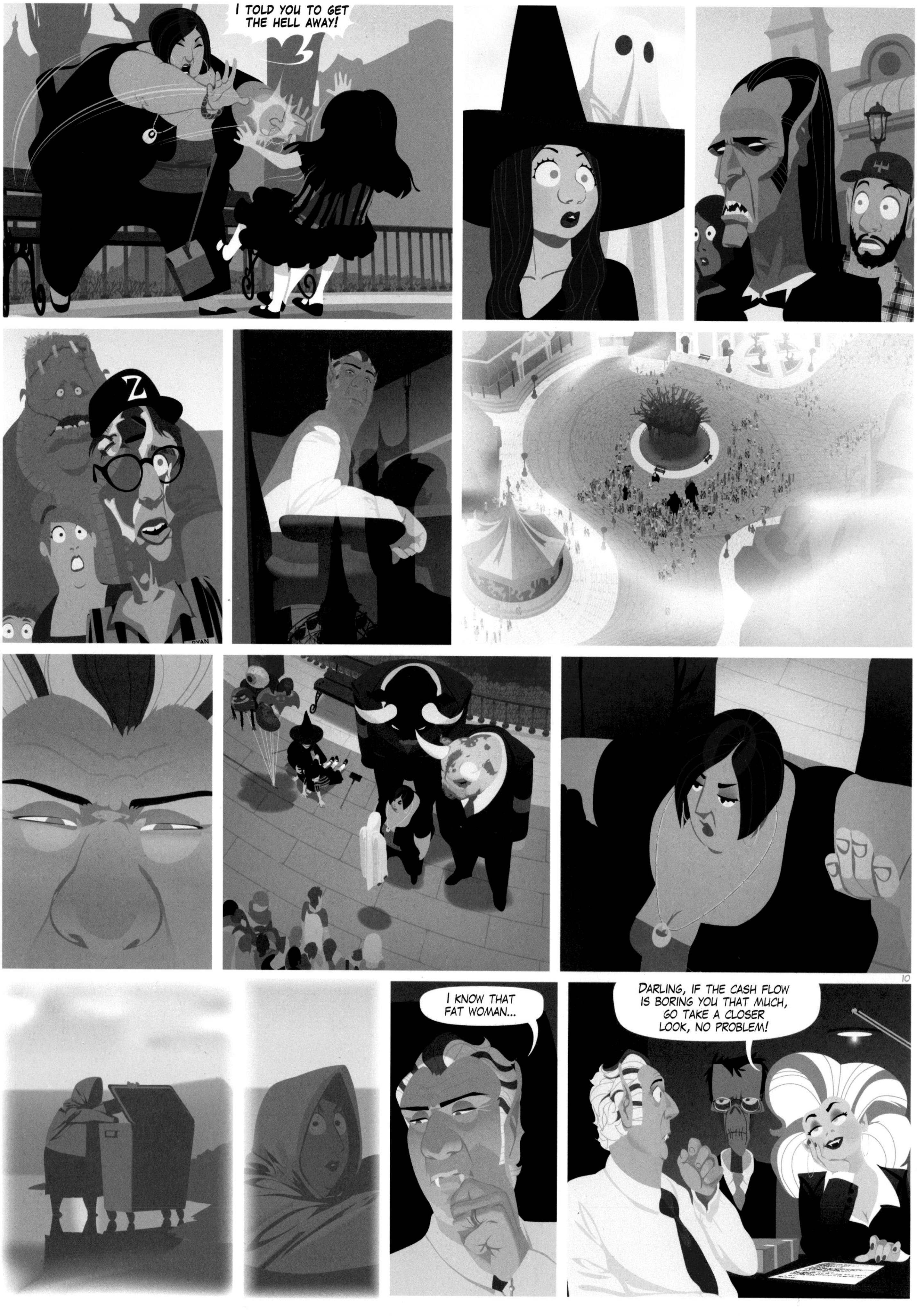
I TOLD YOU TO GET THE HELL AWAY!
I KNOW THAT FAT WOMAN...
DARLING, IF THE CASH FLOW IS BORING YOU THAT MUCH, GO TAKE A CLOSER LOOK, NO PROBLEM!

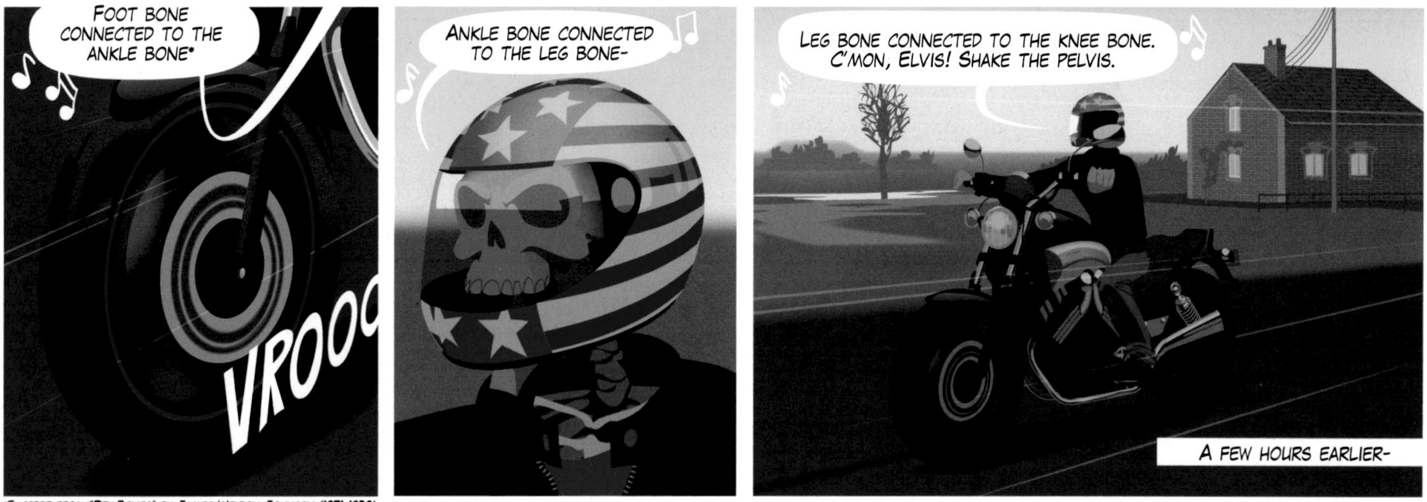
Foot bone connected to the ankle bone*
VROOO
Ankle bone connected to the leg bone-
Leg bone connected to the knee bone. C'mon, Elvis! Shake the pelvis.
A few hours earlier-

*Excerpt from "Dry Bones" by James Weldon Johnson (1871-1938).

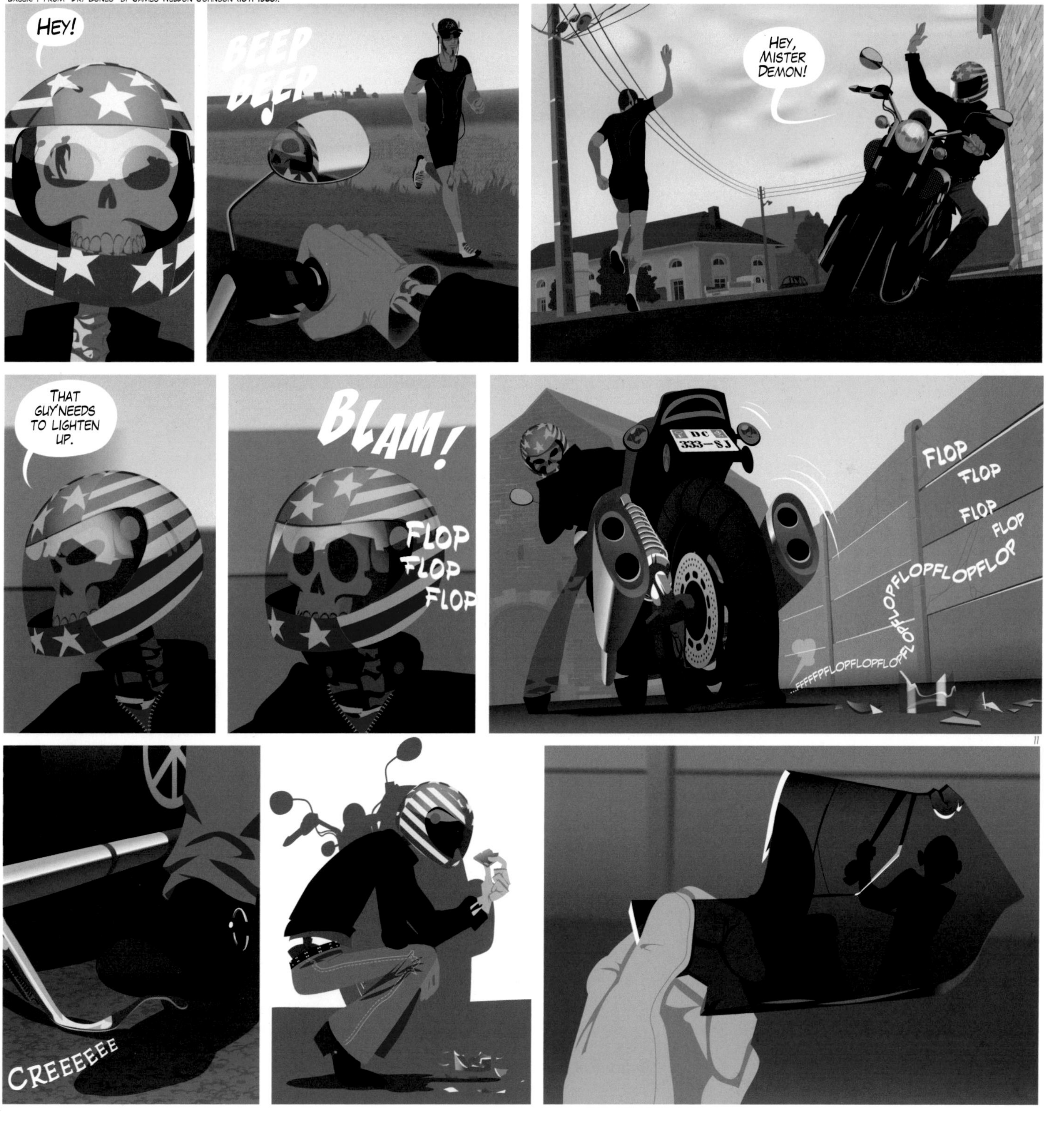
Hey!
BEEP BEEP
Hey, Mister Demon!
That guy needs to lighten up.
BLAM!
FLOP
FLOP
FLOP
DC 333-SJ
FLOP
FLOP
FLOP
FLOP
FLOPFLOPFLOPFLOPFLOP
...FFFFFFFLOPFLOPFLOP
CREEEEEE

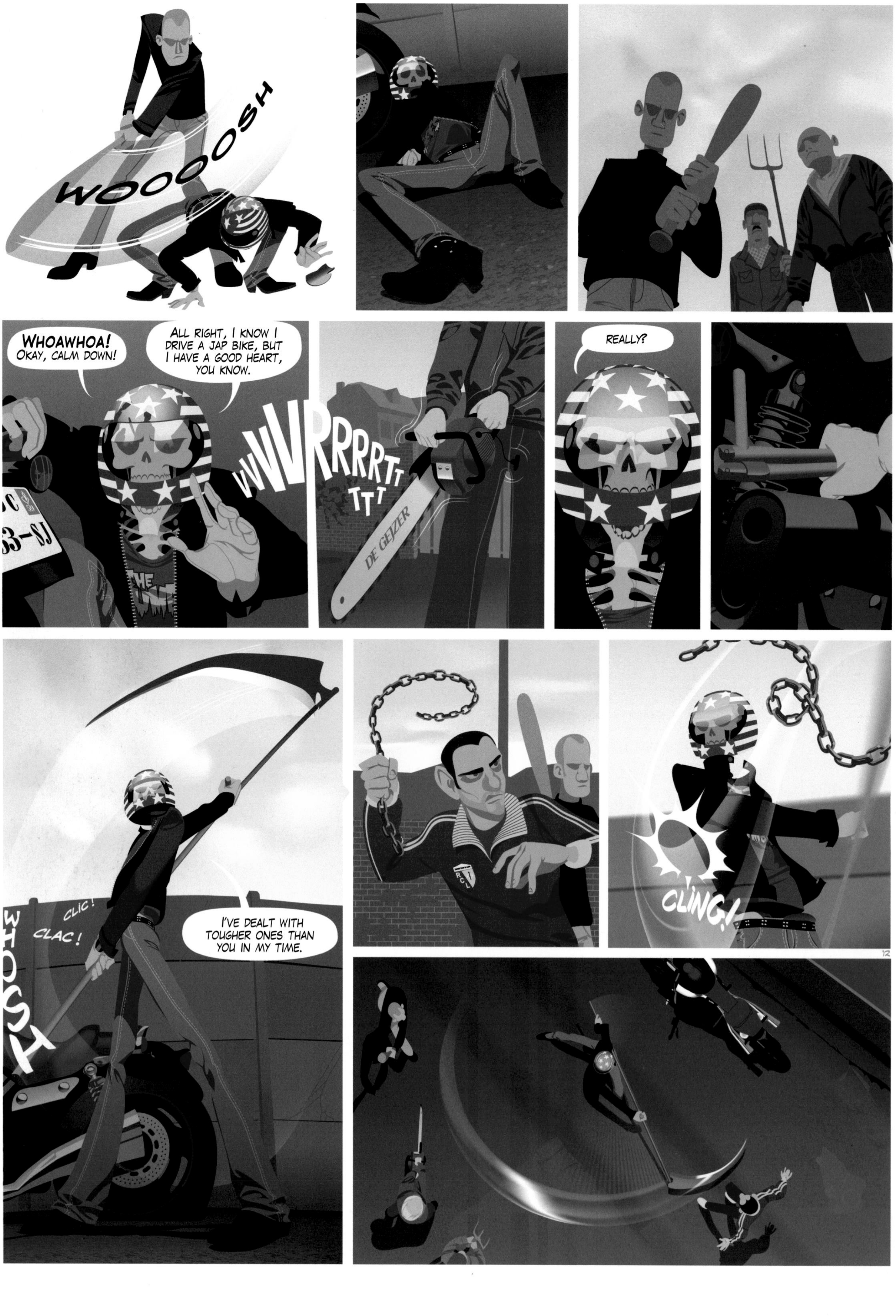
WOOOOSH
WHOAWHOA!
OKAY, CALM DOWN!
ALL RIGHT, I KNOW I DRIVE A JAP BIKE, BUT I HAVE A GOOD HEART, YOU KNOW.
VVVVRRRRRTT TTT
DE GEIZER
REALLY?
CLIC!
CLAC!
I'VE DEALT WITH TOUGHER ONES THAN YOU IN MY TIME.
CLING!
12

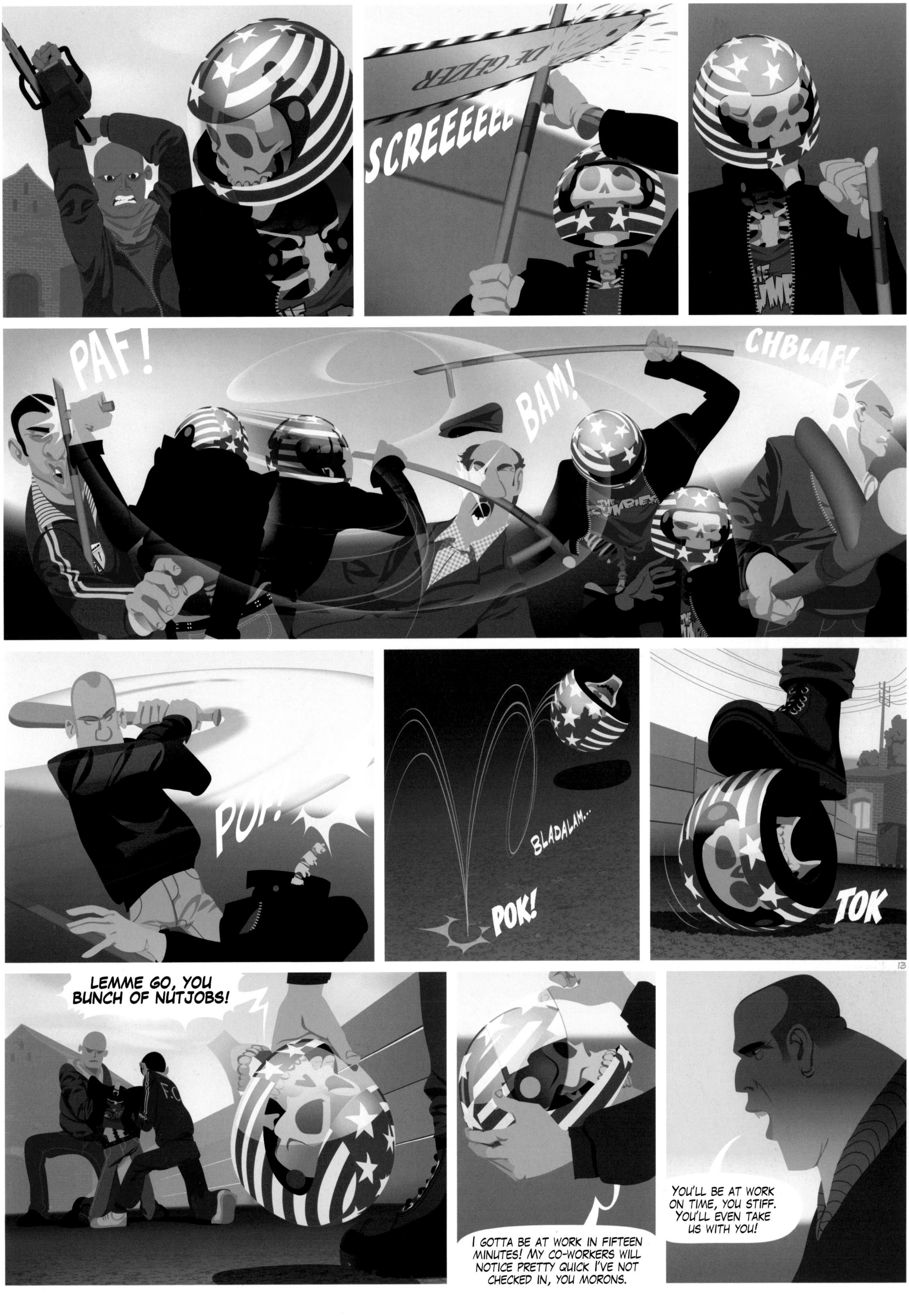
DE GEZER
SCREEEEEE
PAF!
BAM!
CHBLAF!
POP!
BLADALAM...
POK!
TOK
13
LEMME GO, YOU BUNCH OF NUTJOBS!
I GOTTA BE AT WORK IN FIFTEEN MINUTES! MY CO-WORKERS WILL NOTICE PRETTY QUICK I'VE NOT CHECKED IN, YOU MORONS.
YOU'LL BE AT WORK ON TIME, YOU STIFF. YOU'LL EVEN TAKE US WITH YOU!

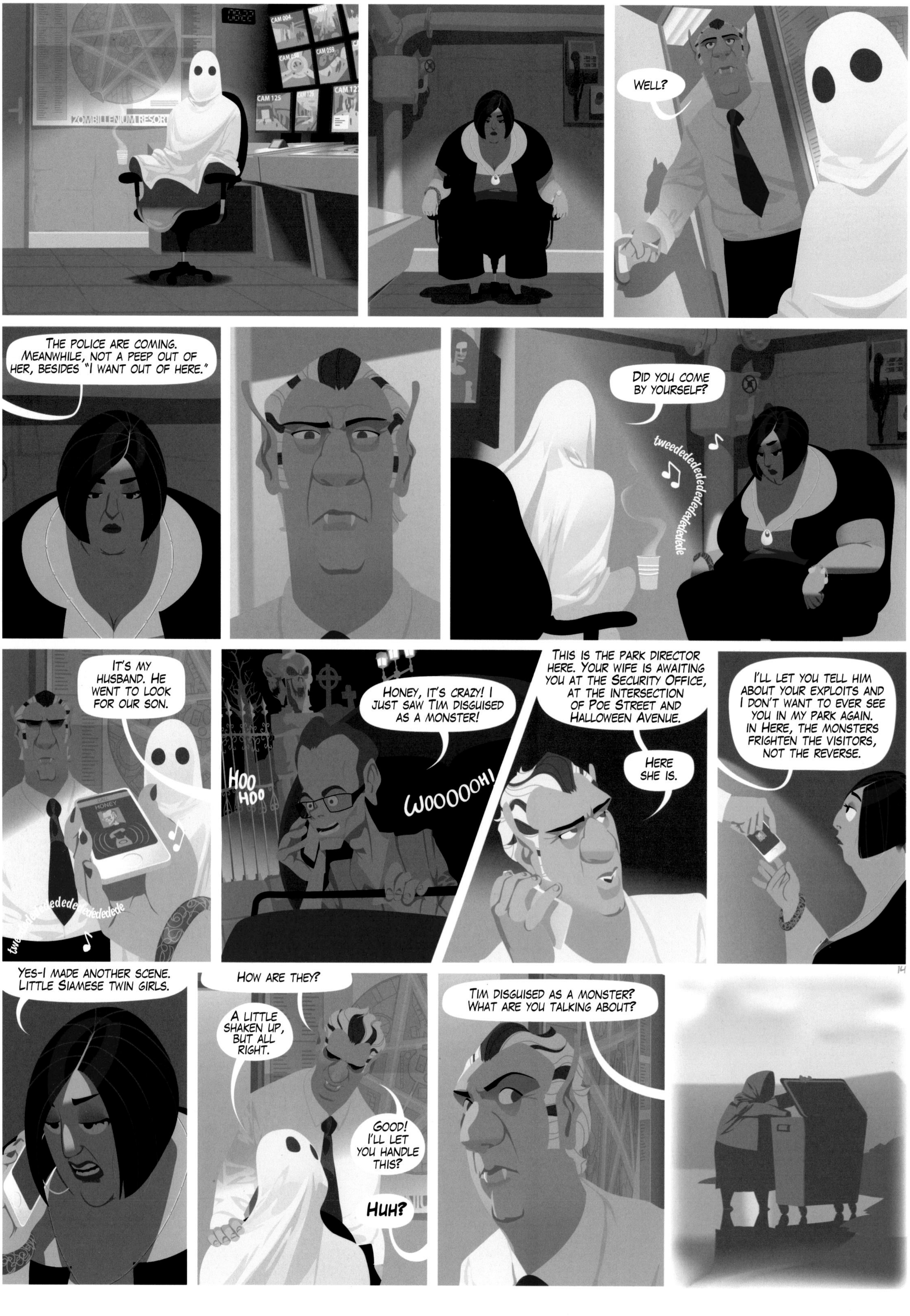
CAM 004
CAM 059
CAM 125
CAM 12
ZOMBILLENIUM RESORT
WELL?
THE POLICE ARE COMING. MEANWHILE, NOT A PEEP OUT OF HER, BESIDES "I WANT OUT OF HERE."
DID YOU COME BY YOURSELF?
tweededededededededede
IT'S MY HUSBAND. HE WENT TO LOOK FOR OUR SON.
HONEY
HONEY, IT'S CRAZY! I JUST SAW TIM DISGUISED AS A MONSTER!
HOO HOO
WOOOOOH!
THIS IS THE PARK DIRECTOR HERE. YOUR WIFE IS AWAITING YOU AT THE SECURITY OFFICE, AT THE INTERSECTION OF POE STREET AND HALLOWEEN AVENUE.
HERE SHE IS.
I'LL LET YOU TELL HIM ABOUT YOUR EXPLOITS AND I DON'T WANT TO EVER SEE YOU IN MY PARK AGAIN. IN HERE, THE MONSTERS FRIGHTEN THE VISITORS, NOT THE REVERSE.
YES-I MADE ANOTHER SCENE. LITTLE SIAMESE TWIN GIRLS.
HOW ARE THEY?
A LITTLE SHAKEN UP, BUT ALL RIGHT.
GOOD! I'LL LET YOU HANDLE THIS?
HUH?
TIM DISGUISED AS A MONSTER? WHAT ARE YOU TALKING ABOUT?

Hi, Boss! You look kinda stressed.

Uh-hello. Anyone have 50 cents?

You drink too much blood, boss. It raises your stress and level of cholesterol.

Hey, do vampires piss blood?

You know, in 3000 years, I've never asked myself that question!

BLOOD O-   MENSES

BLOOD AB+   DROOL FROM A COW IN HEAT

TI···   ···AGE

CO···

I suppose so.

Could they drink it again?

Argh! You are so gross!

BZZZZZ...

GLOOP GLOOP GLOOP

EEEEE EEE

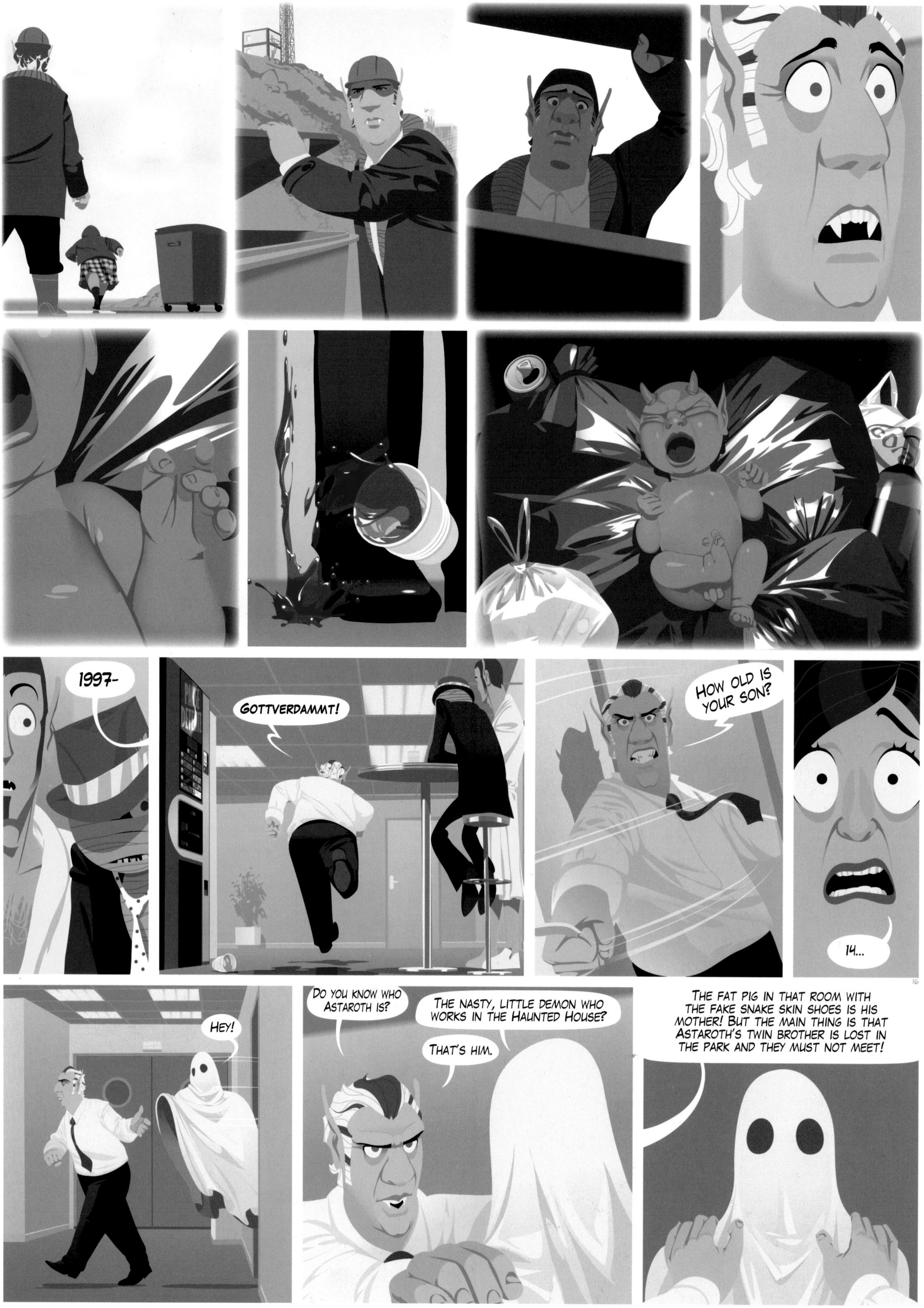
1997-
GOTTVERDAMMT!
HOW OLD IS YOUR SON?
14...
HEY!
DO YOU KNOW WHO ASTAROTH IS?
THE NASTY, LITTLE DEMON WHO WORKS IN THE HAUNTED HOUSE?
THAT'S HIM.
THE FAT PIG IN THAT ROOM WITH THE FAKE SNAKE SKIN SHOES IS HIS MOTHER! BUT THE MAIN THING IS THAT ASTAROTH'S TWIN BROTHER IS LOST IN THE PARK AND THEY MUST NOT MEET!

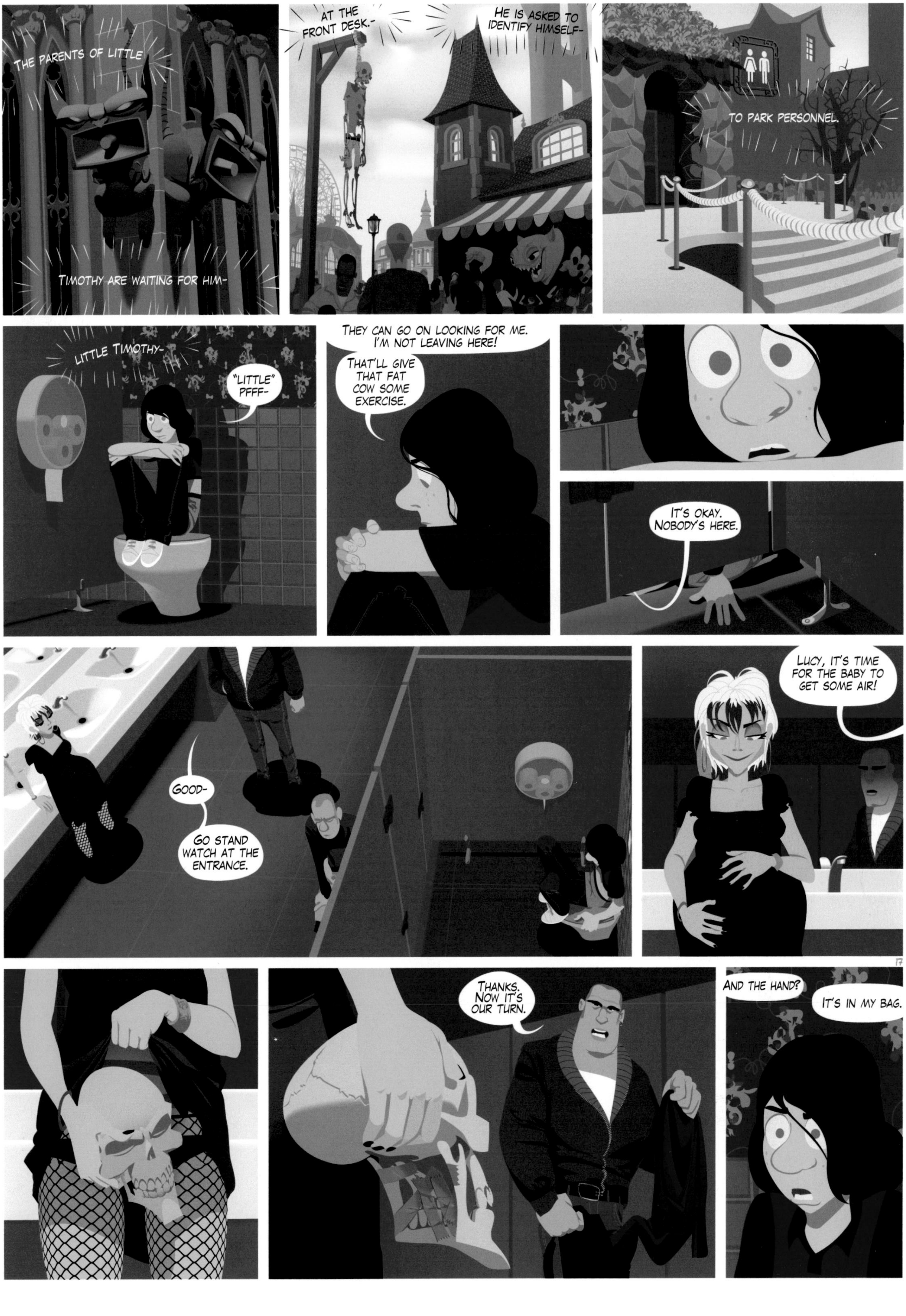

THE PARENTS OF LITTLE
TIMOTHY ARE WAITING FOR HIM-
AT THE FRONT DESK.-
HE IS ASKED TO IDENTIFY HIMSELF-
TO PARK PERSONNEL.
LITTLE TIMOTHY-
"LITTLE" PFFF-
THEY CAN GO ON LOOKING FOR ME. I'M NOT LEAVING HERE!
THAT'LL GIVE THAT FAT COW SOME EXERCISE.
IT'S OKAY. NOBODY'S HERE.
GOOD-
GO STAND WATCH AT THE ENTRANCE.
LUCY, IT'S TIME FOR THE BABY TO GET SOME AIR!
THANKS. NOW IT'S OUR TURN.
AND THE HAND?
IT'S IN MY BAG.

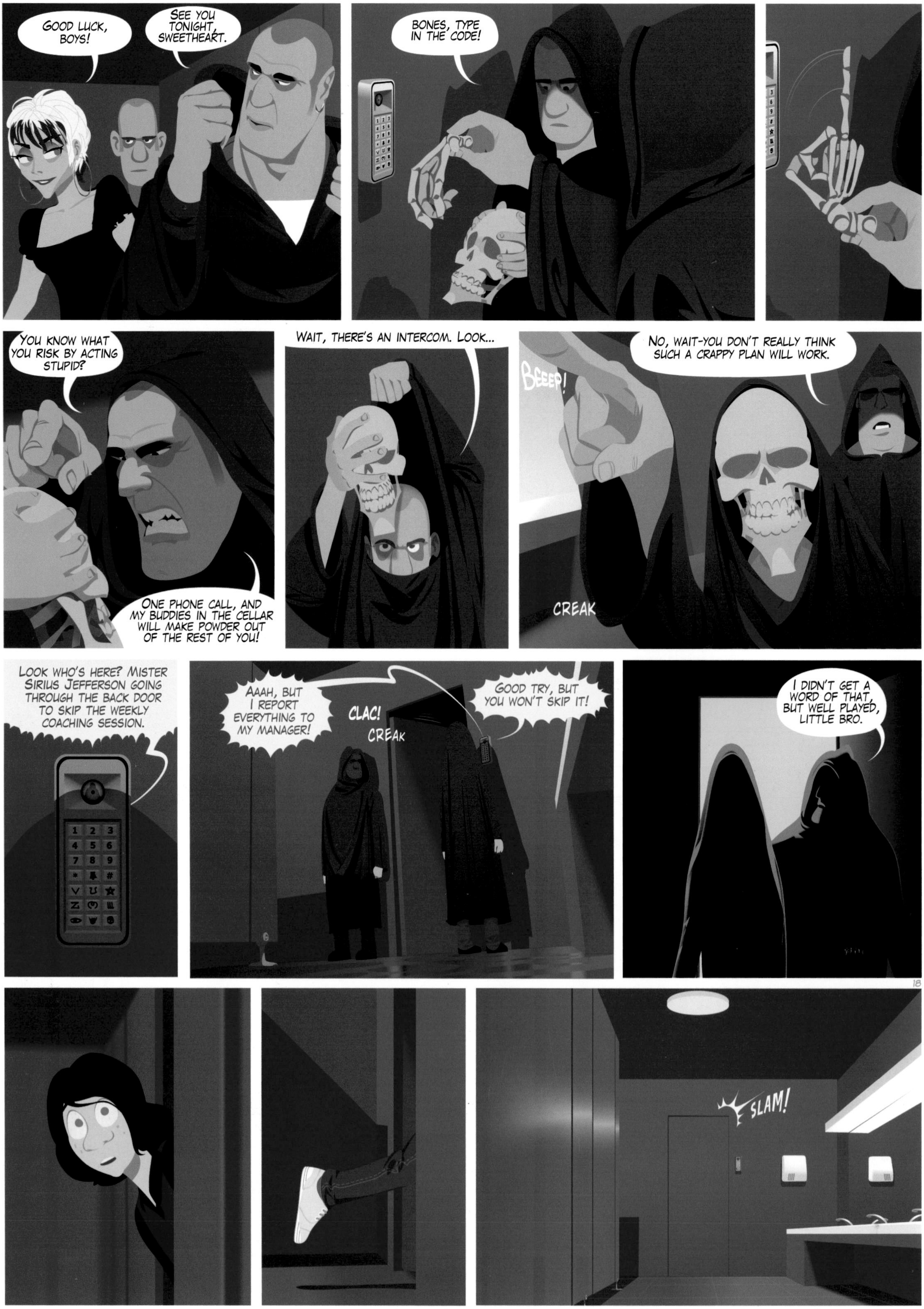
Good luck, boys!
See you tonight, sweetheart.
Bones, type in the code!
You know what you risk by acting stupid?
One phone call, and my buddies in the cellar will make powder out of the rest of you!
Wait, there's an intercom. Look...
BEEEP!
No, wait-you don't really think such a crappy plan will work.
CREAK
Look who's here? Mister Sirius Jefferson going through the back door to skip the weekly coaching session.
Aaah, but I report everything to my manager!
CLAC!
CREAK
Good try, but you won't skip it!
I didn't get a word of that, but well played, little bro.
SLAM!

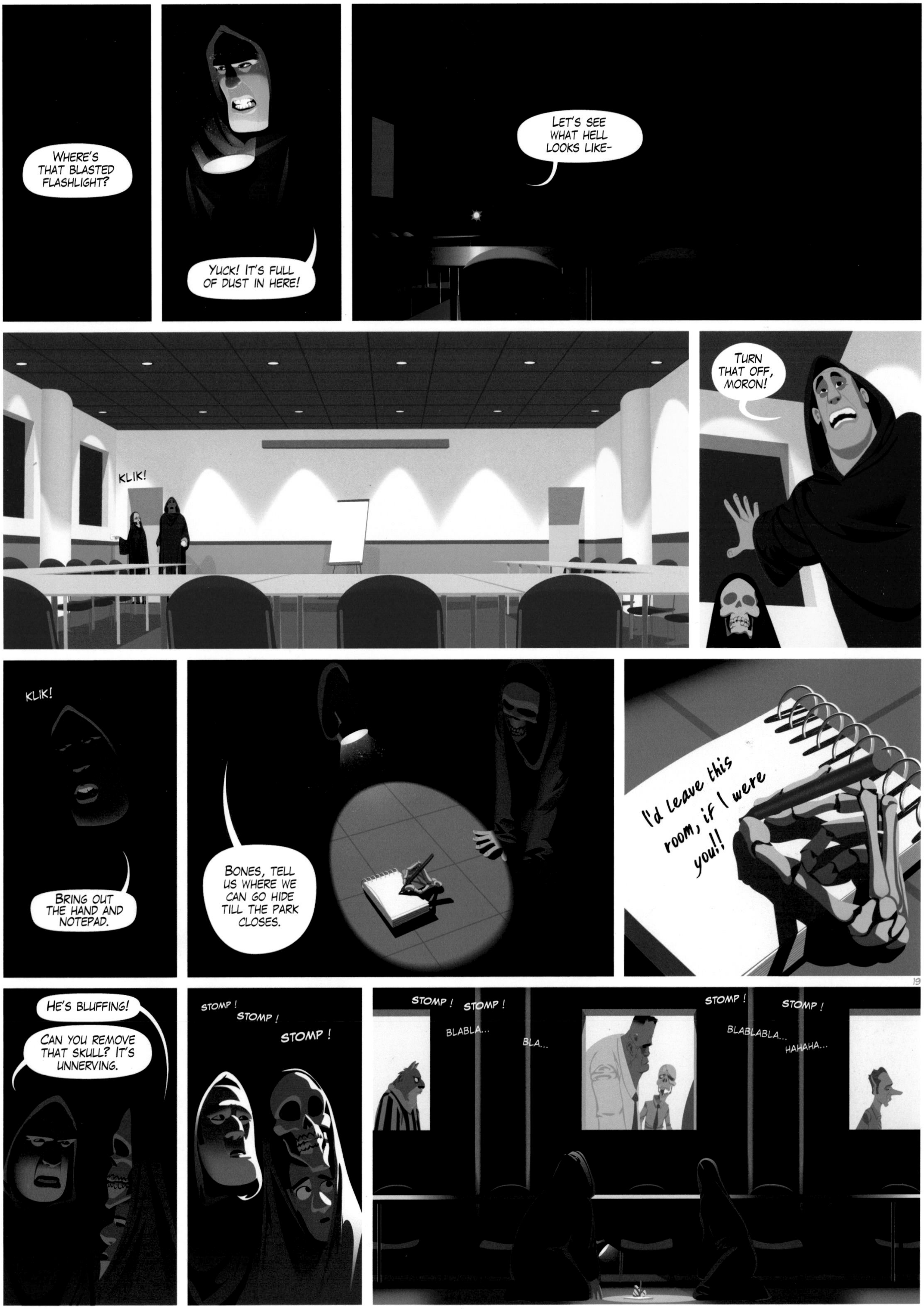
Where's that blasted flashlight?
Yuck! It's full of dust in here!
Let's see what hell looks like-
KLIK!
Turn that off, moron!
KLIK!
Bring out the hand and notepad.
Bones, tell us where we can go hide till the park closes.
I'd leave this room, if I were you!!
He's bluffing!
Can you remove that skull? It's unnerving.
STOMP! STOMP! STOMP!
STOMP! STOMP!
BLABLA...
BLA...
STOMP! STOMP!
BLABLABLA...
HAHAHA...

CLICK!

HEY! WE ALREADY HAVE TWO EARLY BIRDS!

HI, SIRIUS.

SO? KISSING UP?

OKAY, WE CAN GET STARTED.

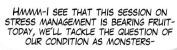

HOW'S IT BEEN SINCE THE LAST TIME?

HMMM-I SEE THAT THIS SESSION ON STRESS MANAGEMENT IS BEARING FRUIT-TODAY, WE'LL TACKLE THE QUESTION OF OUR CONDITION AS MONSTERS-

OR HOW TO CHANNEL OUR DEATH WISH-

TO TRANSFORM IT INTO CREATIVE ENERGY. IT'S CALLED "POSITIVE FREAKISHNESS".

POSITIVE? FREAKISHNESS?

YEAH, HANG WITH ME HERE. THE CIRCLE I'M TRACING REPRESENTS YOUR MURDEROUS INSTINCT.

THIS SECOND CIRCLE IS WHAT I CALL THE "ZONE OF SOCIABILITY." AND AT THE INTERSECTION-

SIR?

YES, ASTAROTH?

WHY AREN'T WE ALLOWED TO KILL HUMANS?

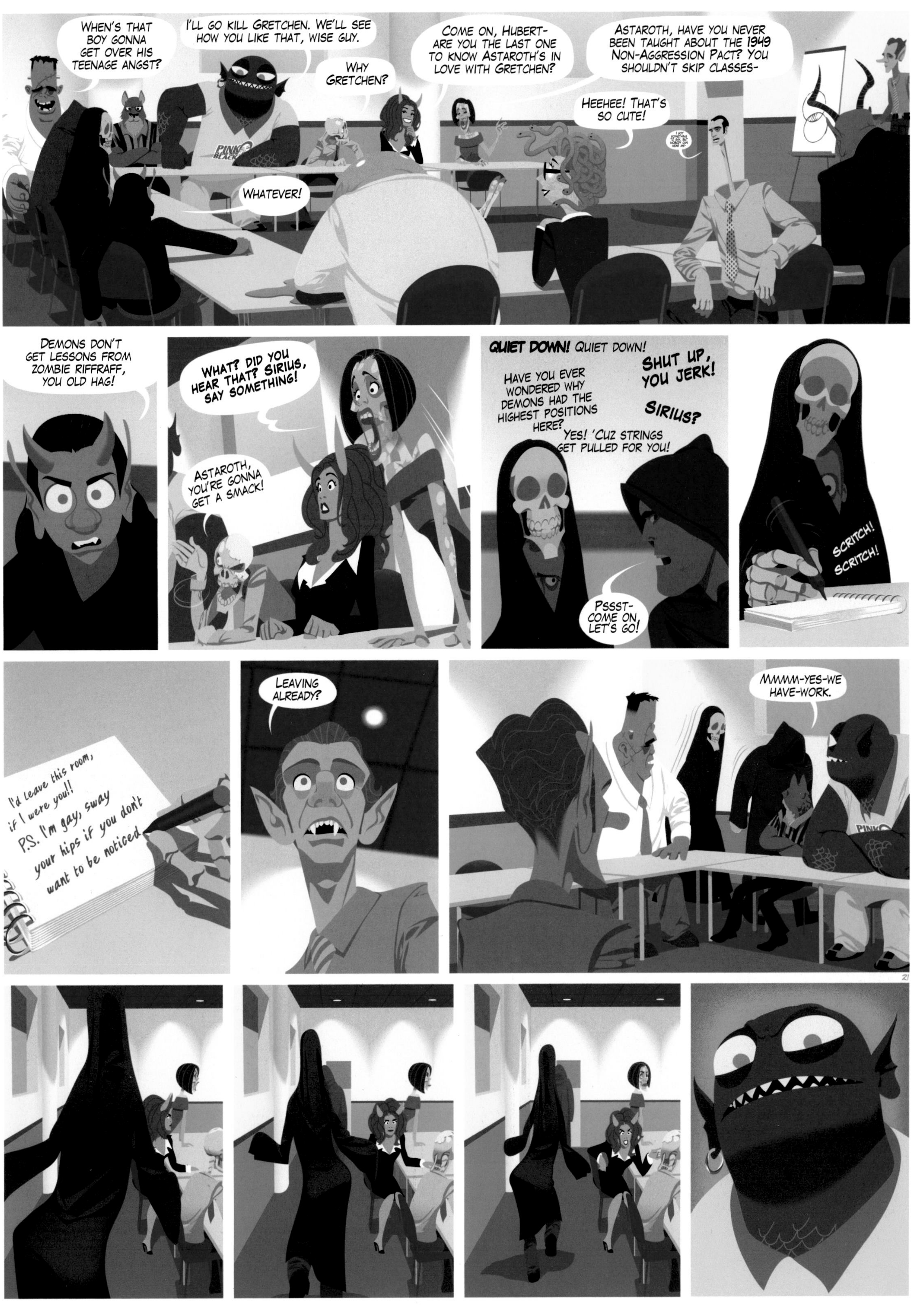

WHEN'S THAT BOY GONNA GET OVER HIS TEENAGE ANGST?
I'LL GO KILL GRETCHEN. WE'LL SEE HOW YOU LIKE THAT, WISE GUY.
WHY GRETCHEN?
COME ON, HUBERT- ARE YOU THE LAST ONE TO KNOW ASTAROTH'S IN LOVE WITH GRETCHEN?
ASTAROTH, HAVE YOU NEVER BEEN TAUGHT ABOUT THE 1949 NON-AGGRESSION PACT? YOU SHOULDN'T SKIP CLASSES-
HEEHEE! THAT'S SO CUTE!
I GOT SOMETHING TO SAY, BUT NOBODY CAN HEAR ME-
WHATEVER!
DEMONS DON'T GET LESSONS FROM ZOMBIE RIFFRAFF, YOU OLD HAG!
WHAT? DID YOU HEAR THAT? SIRIUS, SAY SOMETHING!
ASTAROTH, YOU'RE GONNA GET A SMACK!
QUIET DOWN! QUIET DOWN!
HAVE YOU EVER WONDERED WHY DEMONS HAD THE HIGHEST POSITIONS HERE?
SHUT UP, YOU JERK!
SIRIUS?
YES! 'CUZ STRINGS GET PULLED FOR YOU!
PSSST- COME ON, LET'S GO!
SCRITCH! SCRITCH!
I'd leave this room, if I were you!!
P.S. I'm gay, sway your hips if you don't want to be noticed
LEAVING ALREADY?
MMMM-YES-WE HAVE-WORK.

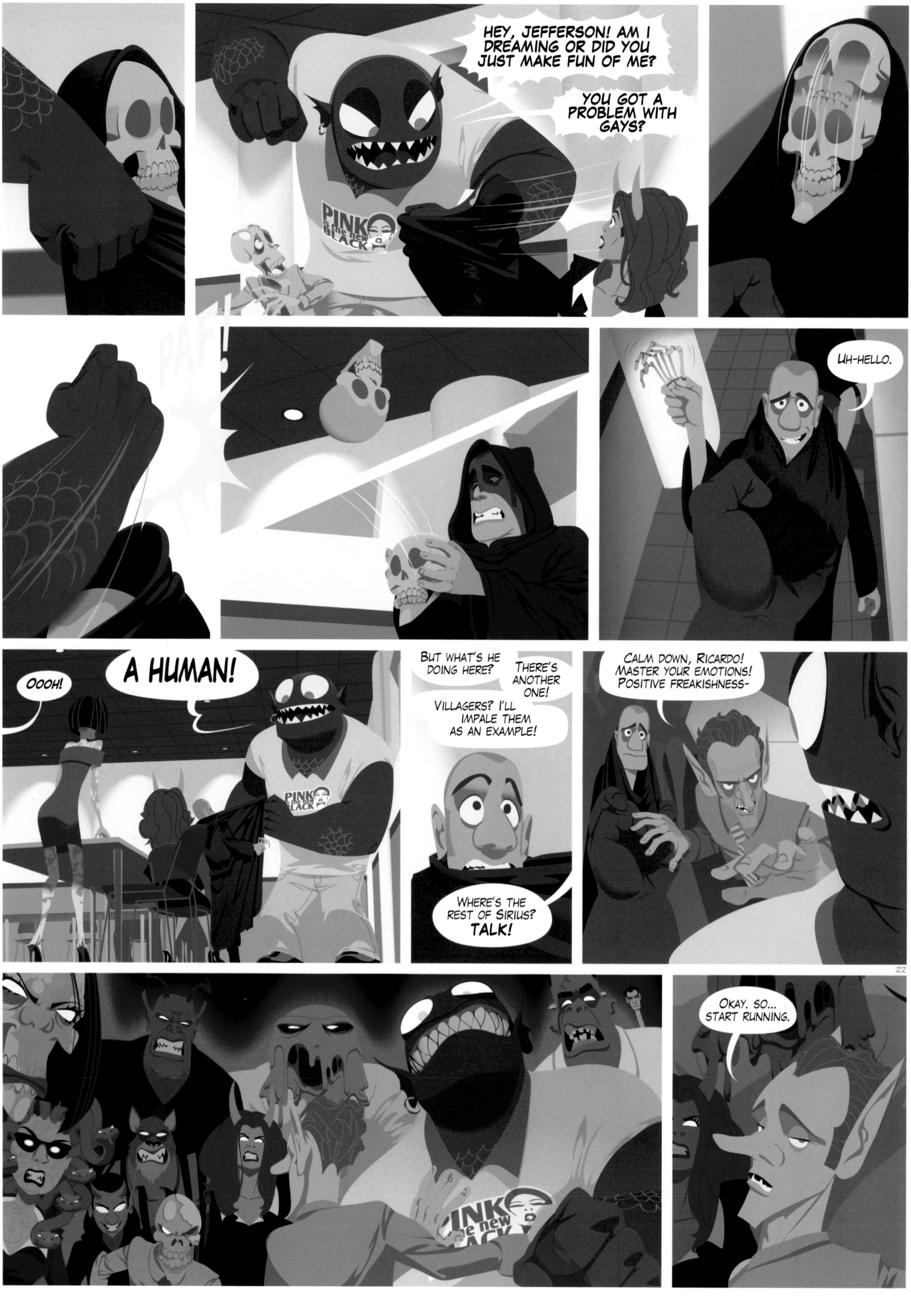

HEY, JEFFERSON! AM I DREAMING OR DID YOU JUST MAKE FUN OF ME?
YOU GOT A PROBLEM WITH GAYS?
PINK is the new BLACK
PAF!
UH-HELLO.
OOOH!
A HUMAN!
PINK is the new BLACK
BUT WHAT'S HE DOING HERE?
THERE'S ANOTHER ONE!
VILLAGERS? I'LL IMPALE THEM AS AN EXAMPLE!
WHERE'S THE REST OF SIRIUS? TALK!
CALM DOWN, RICARDO! MASTER YOUR EMOTIONS! POSITIVE FREAKISHNESS-
OKAY. SO... START RUNNING.

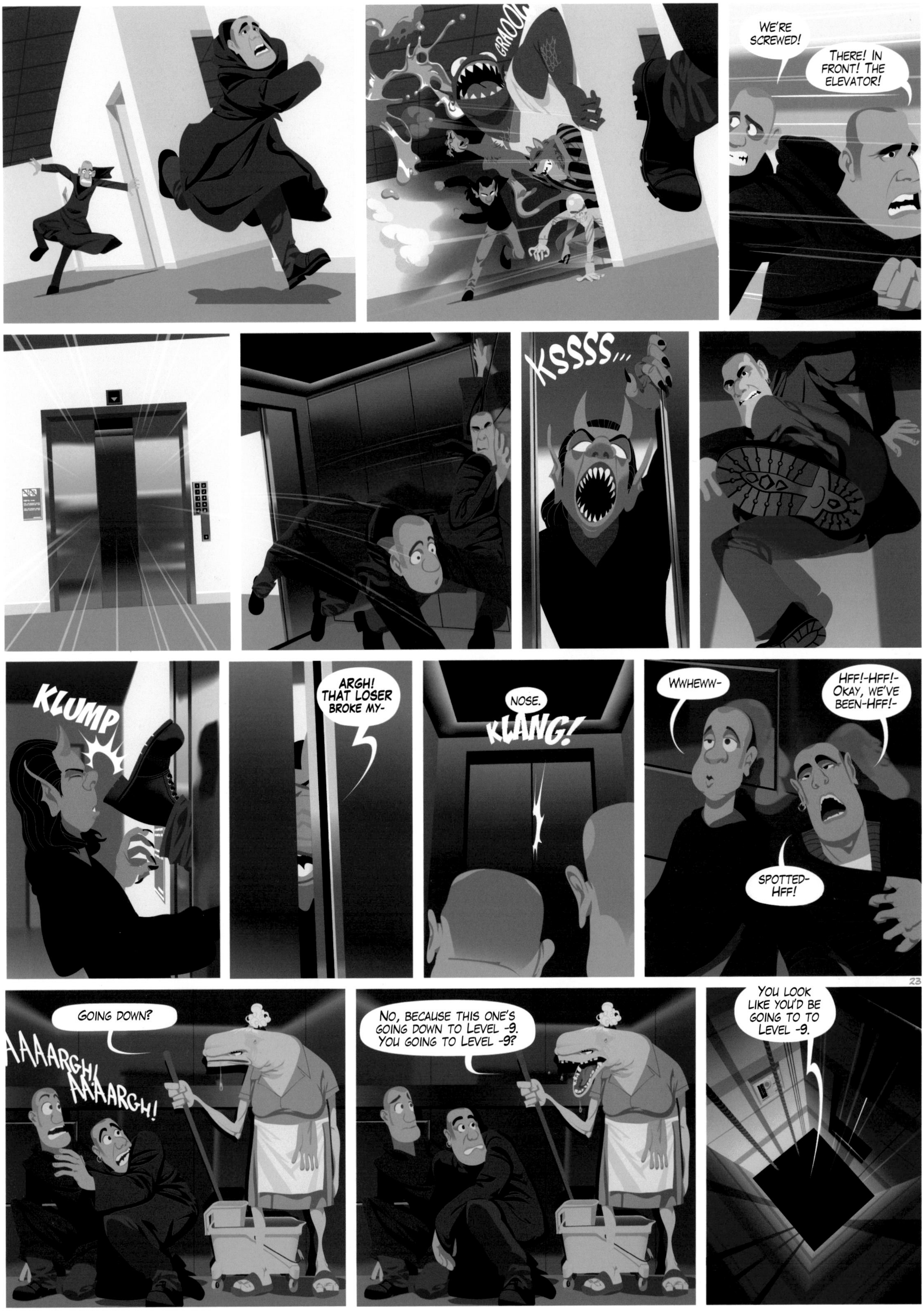
GRAOOO
WE'RE SCREWED!
THERE! IN FRONT! THE ELEVATOR!
KSSSS...
KLUMP
ARGH! THAT LOSER BROKE MY-
NOSE.
KLANG!
WWHEWW-
HFF!-HFF!- OKAY, WE'VE BEEN-HFF!-
SPOTTED-HFF!
GOING DOWN?
AAAARGH!
AAAARGH!
NO, BECAUSE THIS ONE'S GOING DOWN TO LEVEL -9. YOU GOING TO LEVEL -9?
YOU LOOK LIKE YOU'D BE GOING TO TO LEVEL -9.

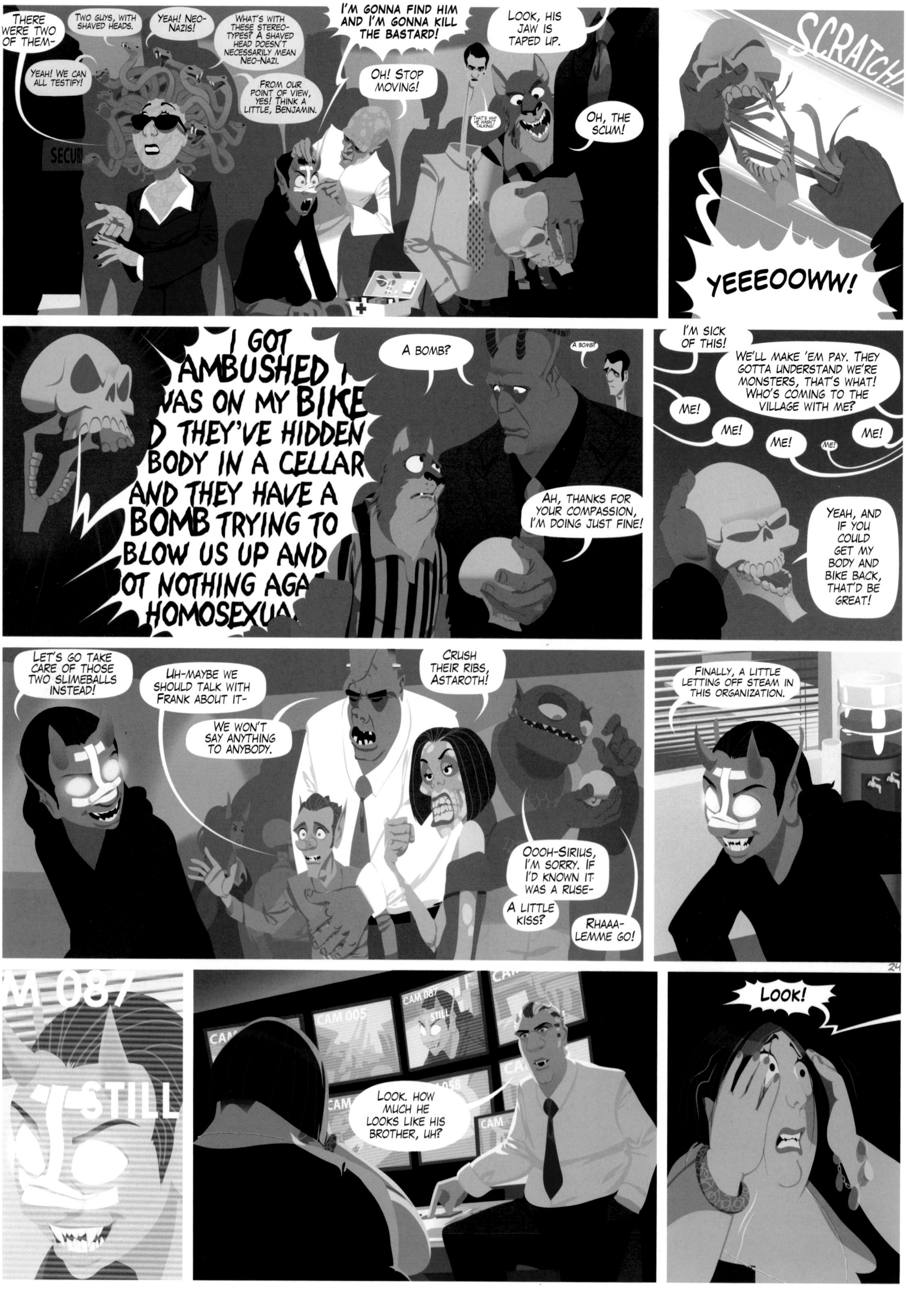

THERE WERE TWO OF THEM-
TWO GUYS, WITH SHAVED HEADS.
YEAH! NEO-NAZIS!
WHAT'S WITH THESE STEREO-TYPES? A SHAVED HEAD DOESN'T NECESSARILY MEAN NEO-NAZI.
YEAH! WE CAN ALL TESTIFY!
FROM OUR POINT OF VIEW, YES! THINK A LITTLE, BENJAMIN.
I'M GONNA FIND HIM AND I'M GONNA KILL THE BASTARD!
OH! STOP MOVING!
LOOK, HIS JAW IS TAPED UP.
THAT'S WHY HE WASN'T TALKING!
OH, THE SCUM!
SECURI
SCRATCH!
YEEEOOWW!
I GOT AMBUSHED I WAS ON MY BIKE D THEY'VE HIDDEN BODY IN A CELLAR AND THEY HAVE A BOMB TRYING TO BLOW US UP AND OT NOTHING AGA HOMOSEXUA
A BOMB?
A BOMB?
AH, THANKS FOR YOUR COMPASSION, I'M DOING JUST FINE!
I'M SICK OF THIS!
WE'LL MAKE 'EM PAY. THEY GOTTA UNDERSTAND WE'RE MONSTERS, THAT'S WHAT! WHO'S COMING TO THE VILLAGE WITH ME?
ME!
ME!
ME!
ME!
ME!
YEAH, AND IF YOU COULD GET MY BODY AND BIKE BACK, THAT'D BE GREAT!
LET'S GO TAKE CARE OF THOSE TWO SLIMEBALLS INSTEAD!
UH-MAYBE WE SHOULD TALK WITH FRANK ABOUT IT-
WE WON'T SAY ANYTHING TO ANYBODY.
CRUSH THEIR RIBS, ASTAROTH!
OOOH-SIRIUS, I'M SORRY. IF I'D KNOWN IT WAS A RUSE-
A LITTLE KISS?
RHAAA-LEMME GO!
FINALLY, A LITTLE LETTING OFF STEAM IN THIS ORGANIZATION.
M 087
STILL
CAM 005
CAM 087
STILL
LOOK. HOW MUCH HE LOOKS LIKE HIS BROTHER, UH?
LOOK!

DOGS DON'T MAKE CATS–

AND HUMANS MAKE MONSTERS EVEN LESS. HOW DO YOU EXPLAIN ALL THIS?

FIFTEEN YEARS AGO, I FOUND OUT I WAS PREGNANT, AFTER FOUR AND A HALF MONTHS, IT WAS TOO LATE TO GET RID OF THE CHILD I DIDN'T WANT. I CALLED A RATHER SHIFTY FELLOW...

BUT THE PREGNANCY CONTINUED AND, FOUR MONTHS LATER, I GAVE BIRTH SECRETLY.

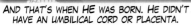

AND THAT'S WHEN HE WAS BORN. HE DIDN'T HAVE AN UMBILICAL CORD OR PLACENTA.

HMM–A WIFI?

HUH?

NOTHING. GO ON.

I PUT HIM IN A DUMPSTER NEAR THE CONSTRUCTION SITE. A MAN CAME UP. THAT WAS YOU, WASN'T IT? I LEFT WITHOUT KNOWING TIM WAS STILL IN MY WOMB. HE WAS BORN "LEGALLY" A FEW HOURS LATER.

25

TIM RAN AWAY IN THE PARK BECAUSE I'M A BAD MOTHER–

BUT IT'S BECAUSE EVERY TIME I LOOK AT HIM...

I SEE THE OTHER ONE, THE ONE WHO BLAMES ME FOR ABANDONING HIM.

SNIFF–

PLEASE, DON'T TELL MY HUSBAND ANYTHING.

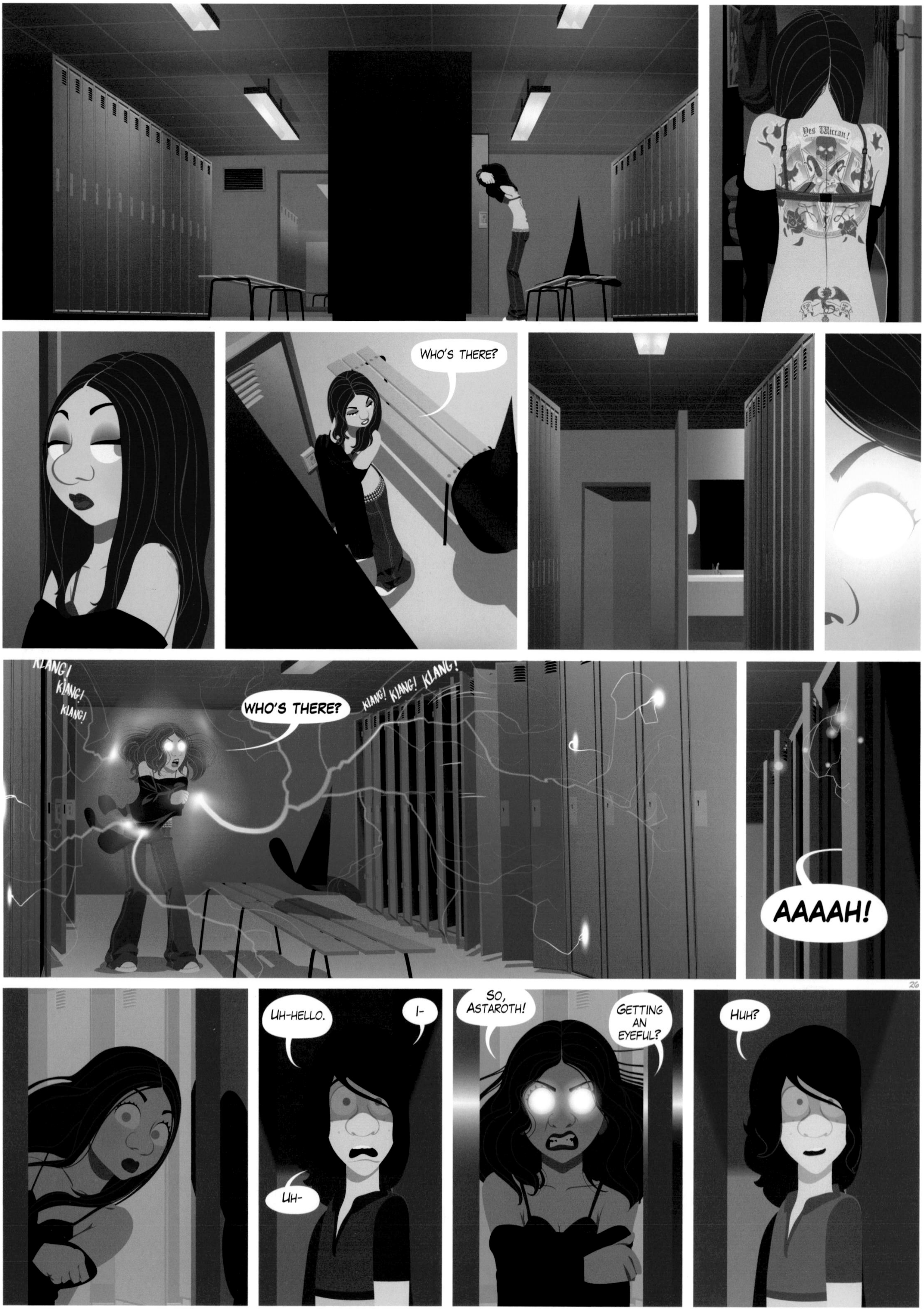
Yes Wiccan!
WHO'S THERE?
KLANG! KLANG! KLANG!
WHO'S THERE?
KLANG! KLANG! KLANG!
AAAAH!
UH-HELLO.
I-
UH-
SO, ASTAROTH!
GETTING AN EYEFUL?
HUH?

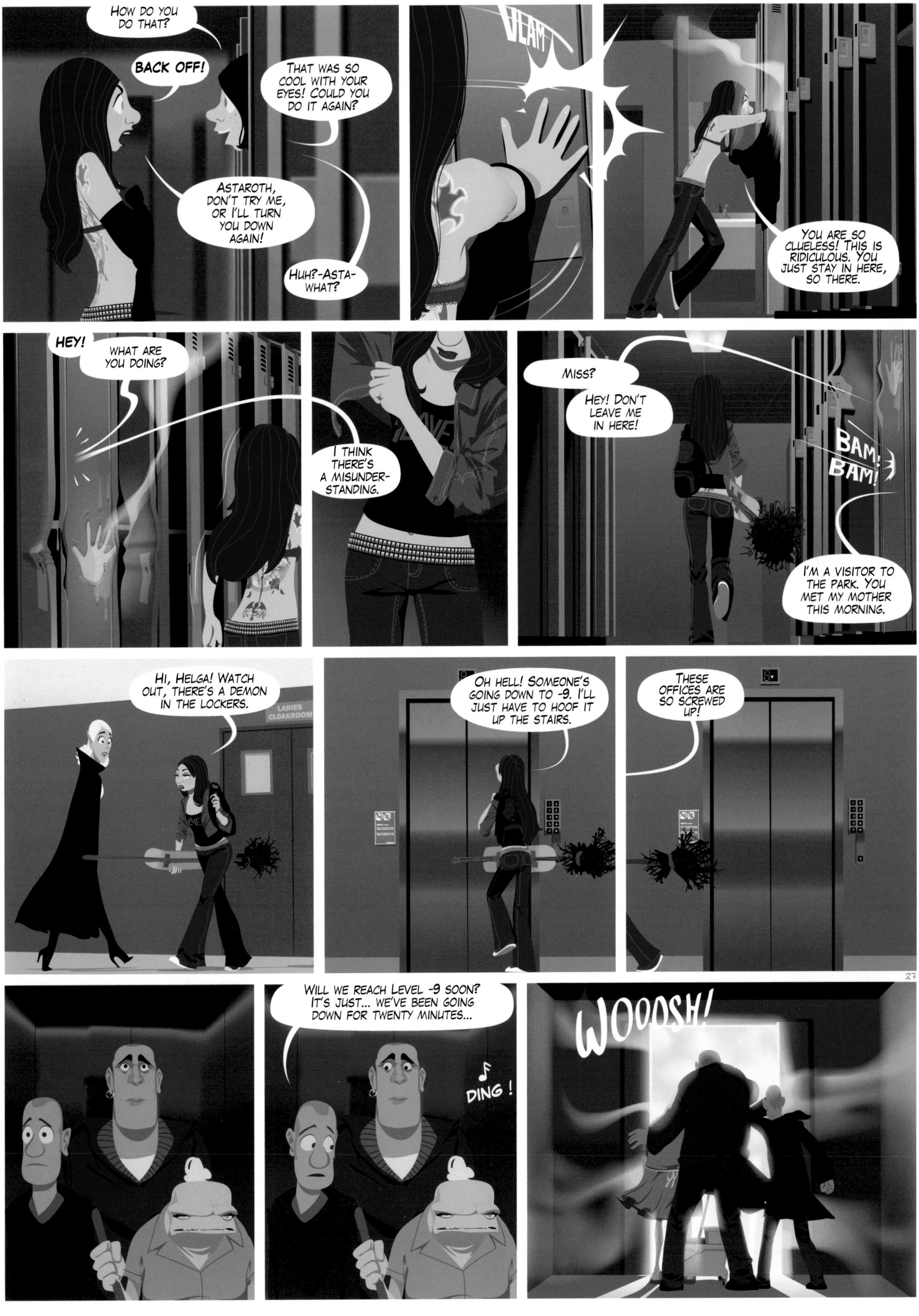

How do you do that?
BACK OFF!
That was so cool with your eyes! Could you do it again?
Astaroth, don't try me, or I'll turn you down again!
Huh?-Asta-what?
VLAM
You are so clueless! This is ridiculous. You just stay in here, so there.
HEY!
What are you doing?
I think there's a misunder-standing.
Miss?
Hey! Don't leave me in here!
BAM! BAM!
I'm a visitor to the park. You met my mother this morning.
Hi, Helga! Watch out, there's a demon in the lockers.
LADIES CLOAKROOM
Oh hell! Someone's going down to -9. I'll just have to hoof it up the stairs.
These offices are so screwed up!
Will we reach Level -9 soon? It's just... we've been going down for twenty minutes...
DING !
WOOOSH!

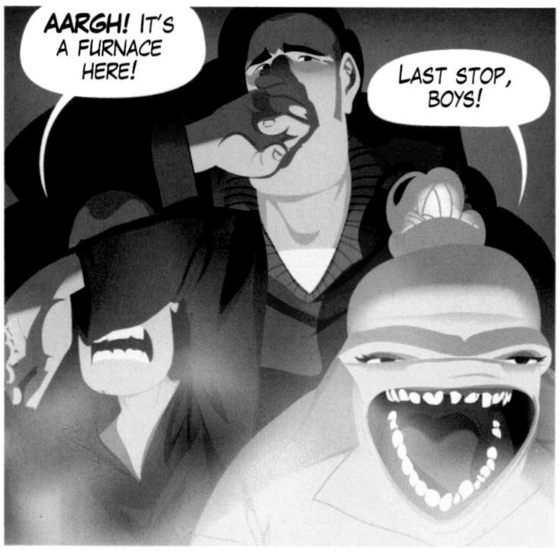
AARGH! IT'S A FURNACE HERE!
LAST STOP, BOYS!

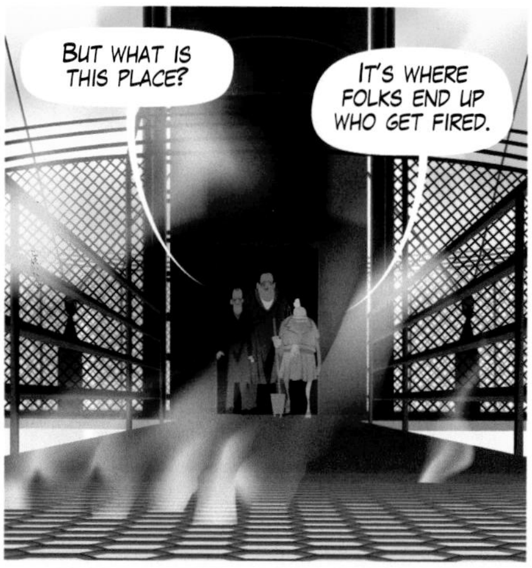
BUT WHAT IS THIS PLACE?
IT'S WHERE FOLKS END UP WHO GET FIRED.

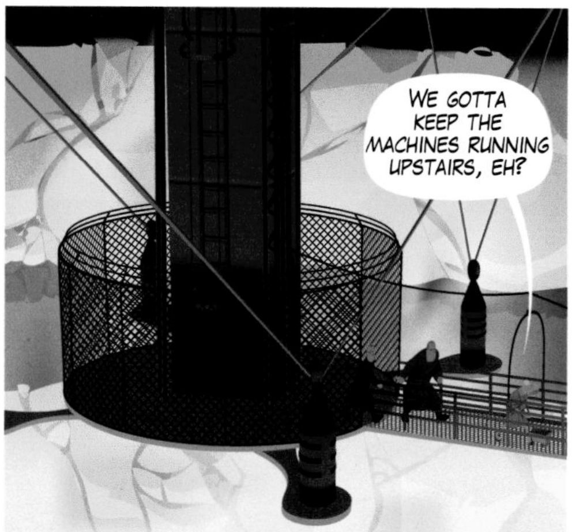
WE GOTTA KEEP THE MACHINES RUNNING UPSTAIRS, EH?

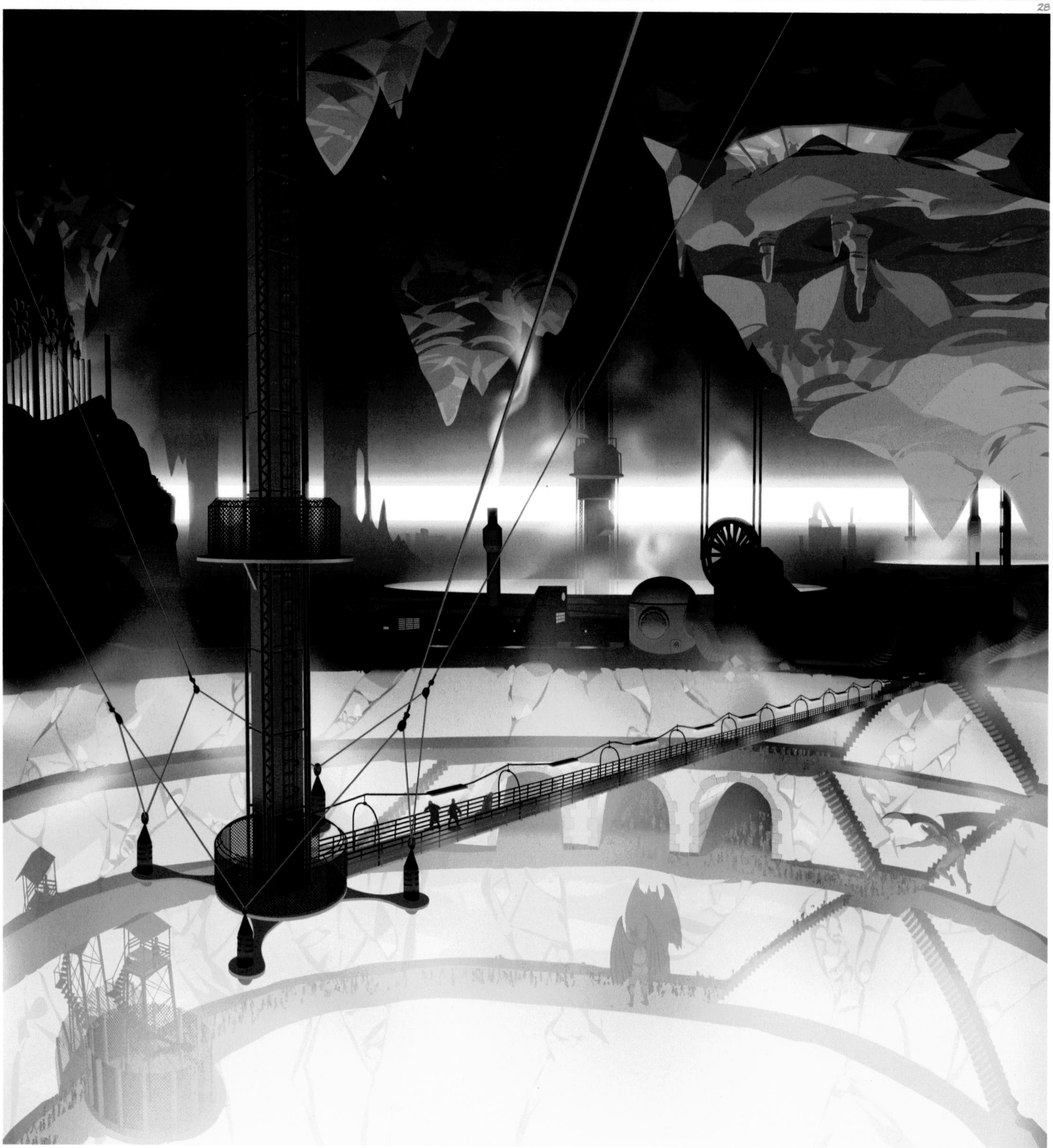

YOUR JOB CONSISTED OF "REINFORCING GROUP COHESION, INSTILLING LOVE FOR THE COMPANY, AND GIVING A SENSE TO LIFE AFTER DEATH." AM I WRONG?

TALENT MANAGEMENT
—
DIRECTOR HUMAN RESOURCES

THAT'S WHAT, WRITTEN IN YOUR CONTRACT FOR BUSINESS COACHING.

THERE WAS PROGRESS-

I'D ORGANIZED A TEAM-BUILDING SEMINAR IN THE CARPATHIANS.

A LIP DUB, TOO.

AT THE MOMENT I'M TALKING TO YOU, SOME OF YOUR "STUDENTS" ARE PLANNING TO ATTACK THE NEIGHBORING VILLAGE-

WHILE THE OTHER PART IS CHASING TWO HUMANS IN THE OFFICES TO MASSACRE THEM.

BUT IT'S PRECISELY BECAUSE OF THOSE HUMANS! YOU KNOW WHAT IT'S LIKE-IT'S LIKE PUTTING RABBITS IN A WOLF ENCLOSURE-

UH-SORRY-

I FAILED.

FAILURE ISN'T AN OPTION.

YOU'RE FIRED.

WE CAN'T KEEP YOU HERE.

SCRIIITCH!

CONTRACT
BETWEEN MR. JEAN-PIERRA DUMOULIN,
AND
Mr. BEHEMOTH,

NO!

NOOOO!

NOOO

OOOO!

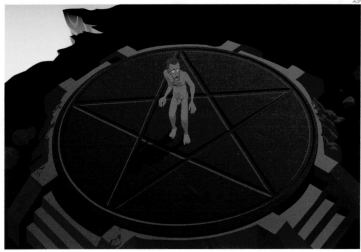

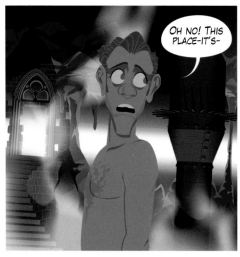

OH NO! THIS PLACE-IT'S-
AAAAH!
2560x1920
ISO AUTO
2560x1920
ISO AUTO
2560x1920
ISO AUTO
I CAN'T BELIEVE IT! HE'S FILMING IT!
WE'RE IN AN AMUSEMENT PARK, AREN'T WE?
LET'S RETURN TO THE ELEVATOR.
TWO SECONDS, I'M SENDING THE VIDEO-
EEEEE
TRICK OR TREAT?

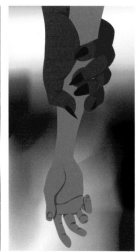

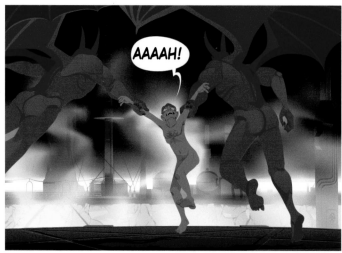

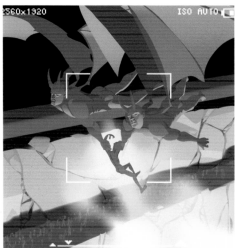

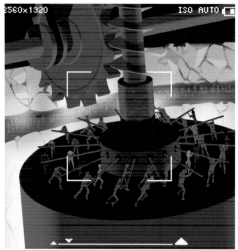

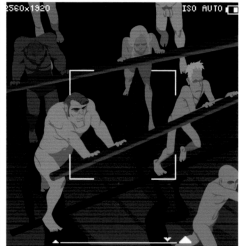

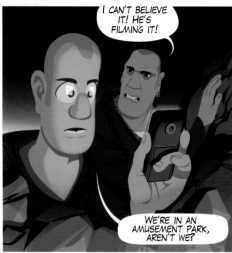

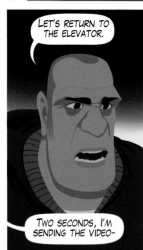

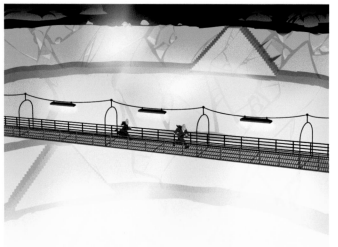

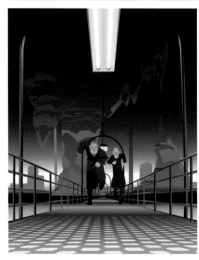

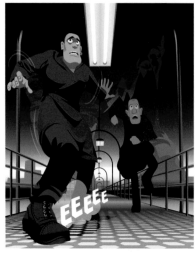

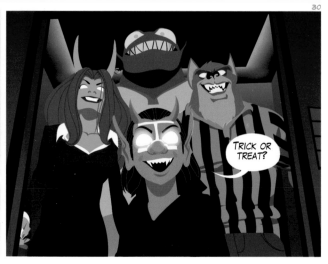

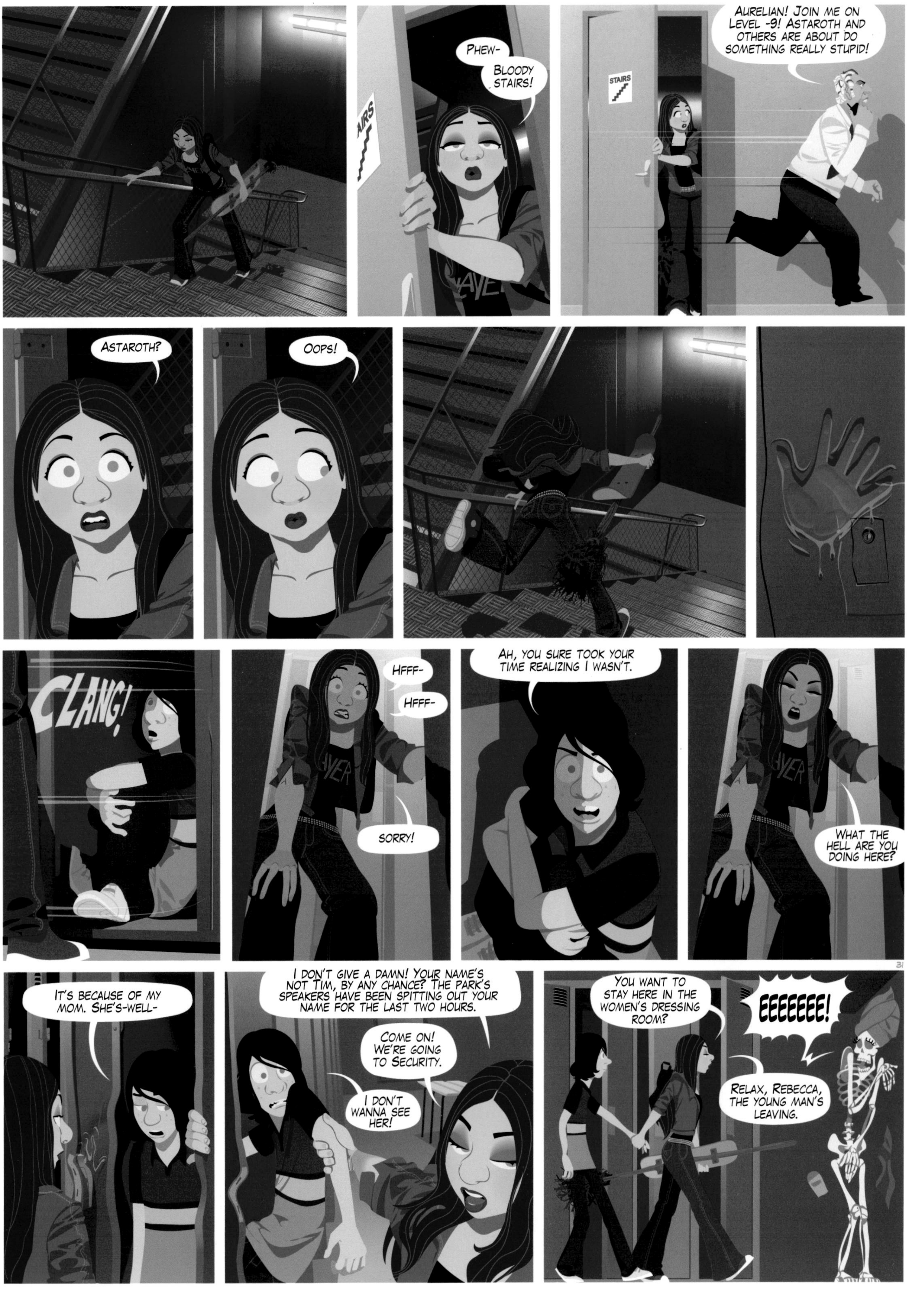

Phew-
Bloody stairs!
STAIRS
Aurelian! Join me on Level -9! Astaroth and others are about do something really stupid!
STAIRS
Astaroth?
Oops!
CLANG!
Hfff-
Hfff-
Sorry!
Ah, you sure took your time realizing I wasn't.
What the hell are you doing here?
It's because of my mom. She's-well-
I don't give a damn! Your name's not Tim, by any chance? The park's speakers have been spitting out your name for the last two hours.
Come on! We're going to Security.
I don't wanna see her!
You want to stay here in the women's dressing room?
EEEEEEE!
Relax, Rebecca, the young man's leaving.

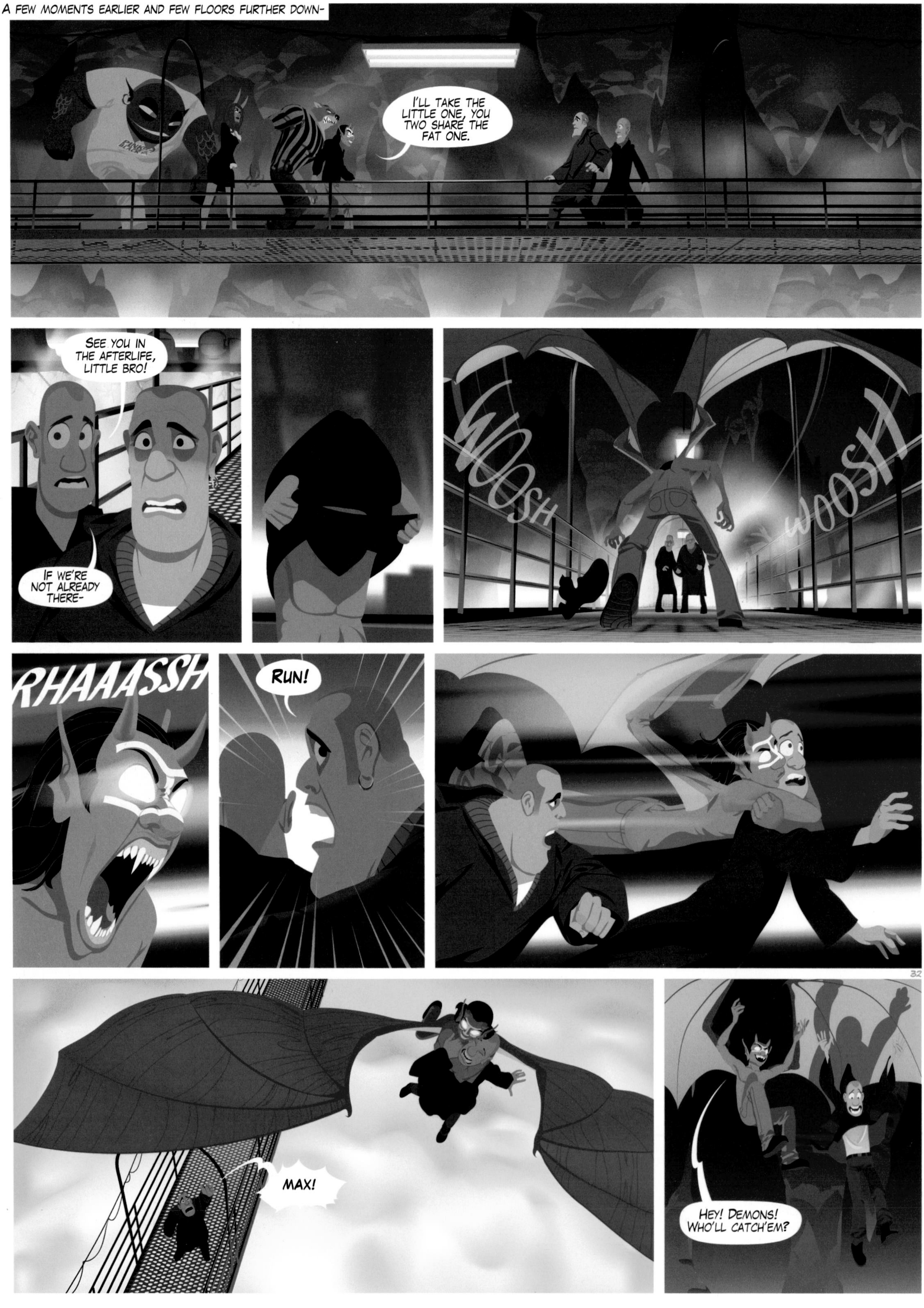
A FEW MOMENTS EARLIER AND FEW FLOORS FURTHER DOWN-
I'LL TAKE THE LITTLE ONE, YOU TWO SHARE THE FAT ONE.
SEE YOU IN THE AFTERLIFE, LITTLE BRO!
IF WE'RE NOT ALREADY THERE-
WOOSH
WOOSH
RHAAASSH
RUN!
MAX!
HEY! DEMONS! WHO'LL CATCH'EM?

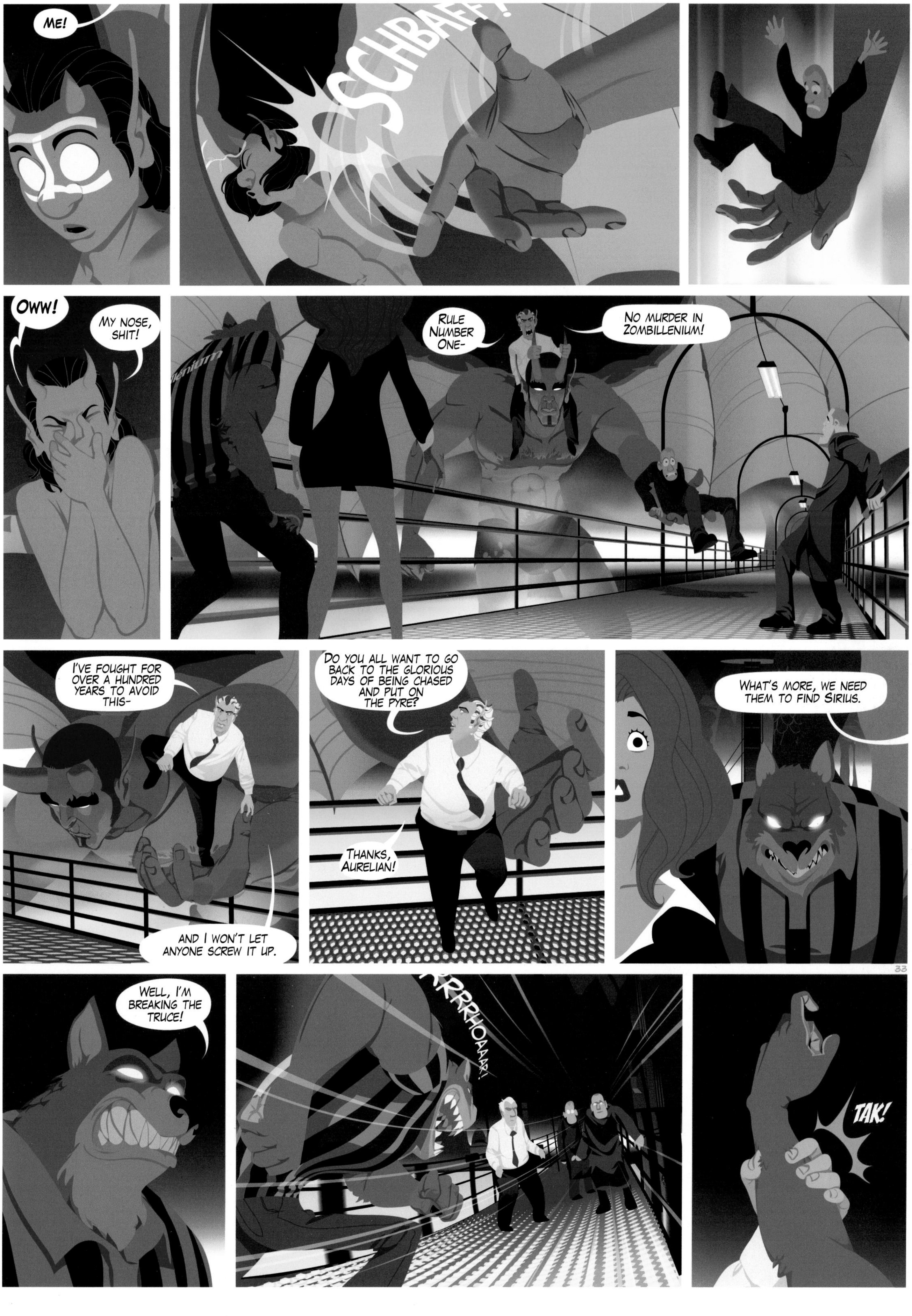
ME!
SCHBAFF!
OWW!
MY NOSE, SHIT!
RULE NUMBER ONE-
NO MURDER IN ZOMBILLENIUM!
I'VE FOUGHT FOR OVER A HUNDRED YEARS TO AVOID THIS-
AND I WON'T LET ANYONE SCREW IT UP.
DO YOU ALL WANT TO GO BACK TO THE GLORIOUS DAYS OF BEING CHASED AND PUT ON THE PYRE?
THANKS, AURELIAN!
WHAT'S MORE, WE NEED THEM TO FIND SIRIUS.
WELL, I'M BREAKING THE TRUCE!
RRRRHOAAAR!
TAK!

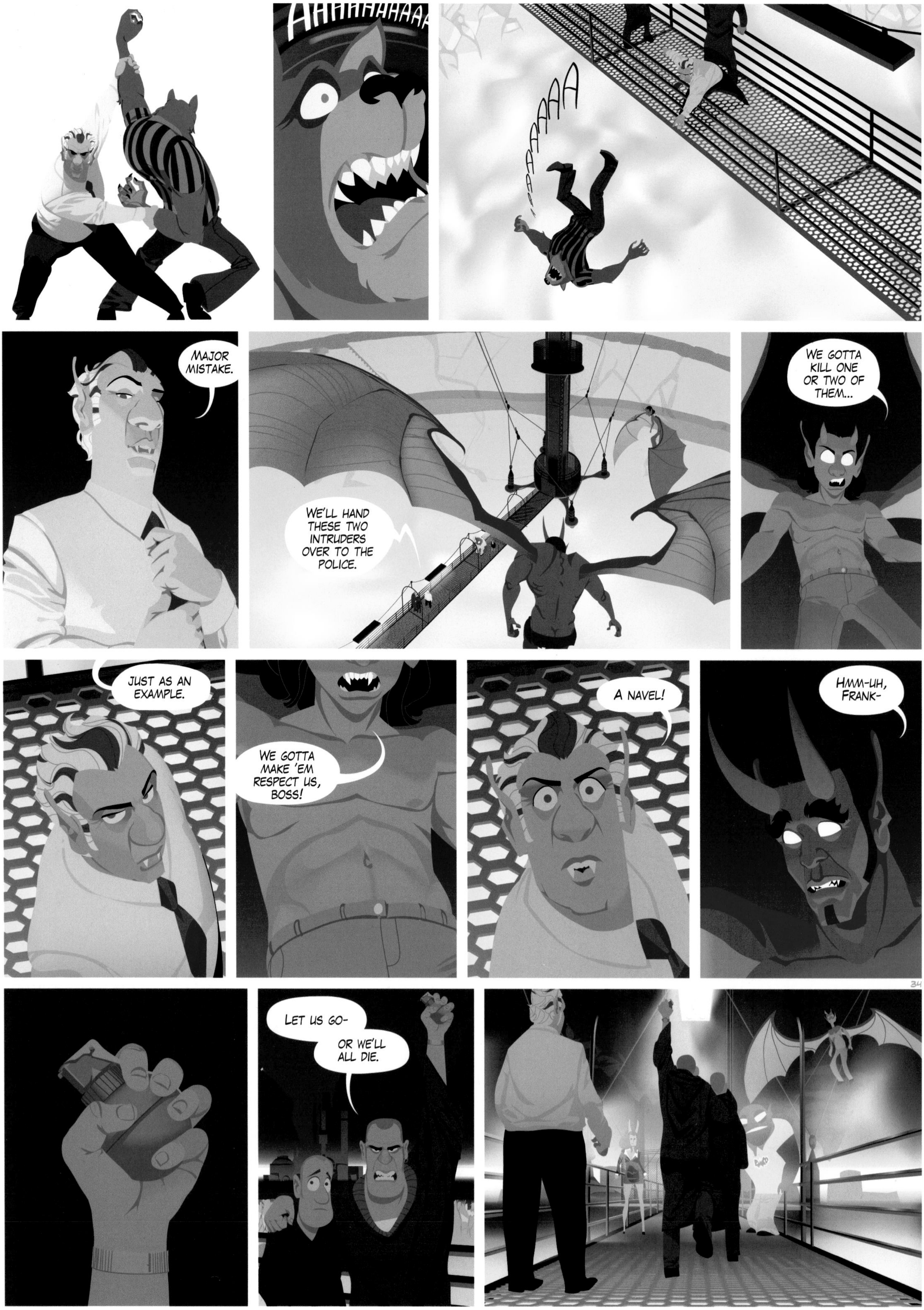
AAAAAAAAAAA
AAAAAAA!
MAJOR MISTAKE.
WE'LL HAND THESE TWO INTRUDERS OVER TO THE POLICE.
WE GOTTA KILL ONE OR TWO OF THEM...
JUST AS AN EXAMPLE.
WE GOTTA MAKE 'EM RESPECT US, BOSS!
A NAVEL!
HMM-UH, FRANK-
LET US GO-
OR WE'LL ALL DIE.

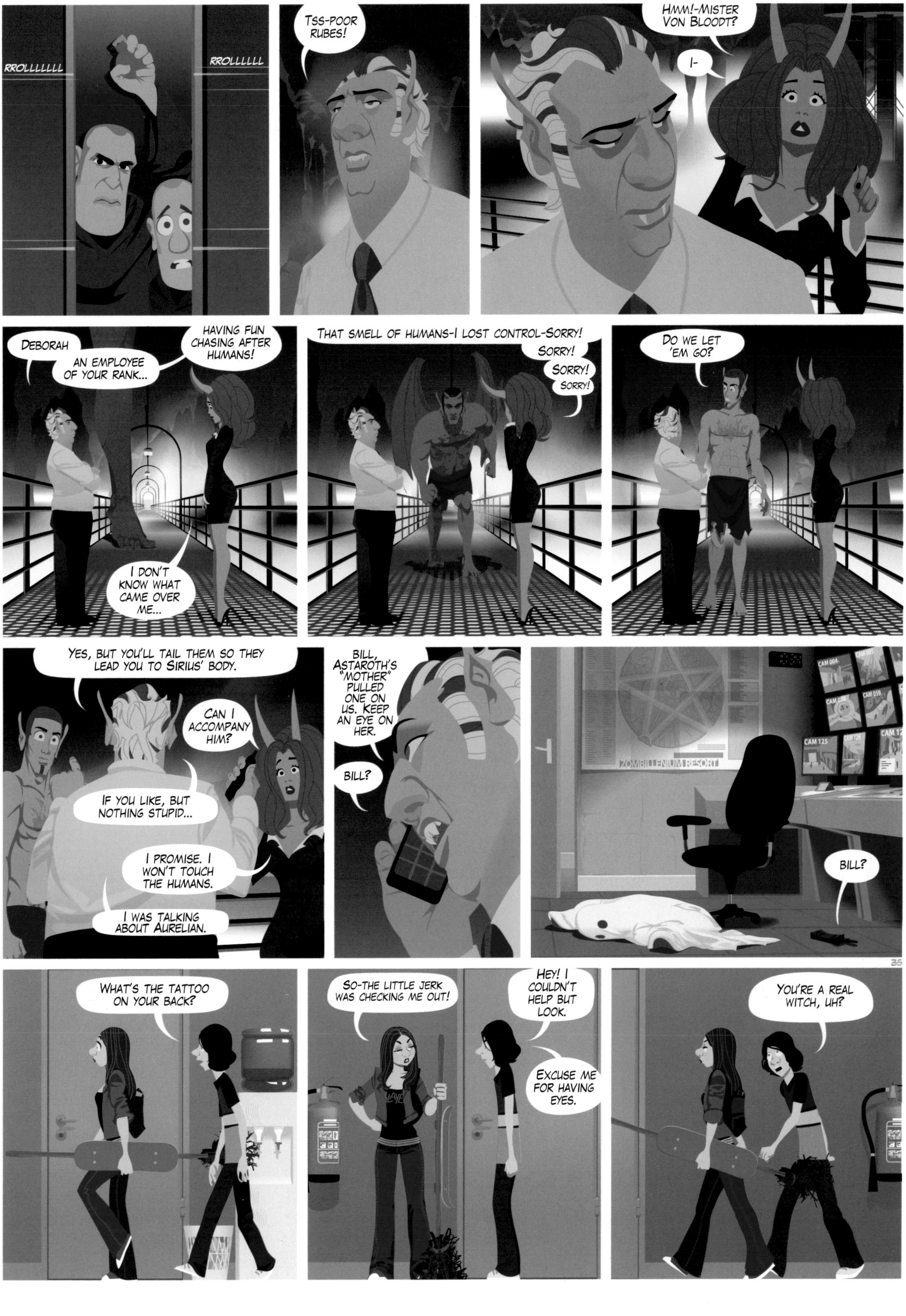
RROLLLLLLL
RROLLLLLL
TSS-POOR RUBES!
HMM!-MISTER VON BLOODT?
I-
DEBORAH
AN EMPLOYEE OF YOUR RANK...
HAVING FUN CHASING AFTER HUMANS!
I DON'T KNOW WHAT CAME OVER ME...
THAT SMELL OF HUMANS-I LOST CONTROL-SORRY!
SORRY!
SORRY!
SORRY!
DO WE LET 'EM GO?
YES, BUT YOU'LL TAIL THEM SO THEY LEAD YOU TO SIRIUS' BODY.
CAN I ACCOMPANY HIM?
IF YOU LIKE, BUT NOTHING STUPID...
I PROMISE. I WON'T TOUCH THE HUMANS.
I WAS TALKING ABOUT AURELIAN.
BILL, ASTAROTH'S "MOTHER" PULLED ONE ON US. KEEP AN EYE ON HER.
BILL?
ZOMBILLENIUM RESORT
CAM 004
CAM 005
CAM 059
CAM 125
CAM 128
BILL?
WHAT'S THE TATTOO ON YOUR BACK?
SO-THE LITTLE JERK WAS CHECKING ME OUT!
HEY! I COULDN'T HELP BUT LOOK.
EXCUSE ME FOR HAVING EYES.
YOU'RE A REAL WITCH, UH?

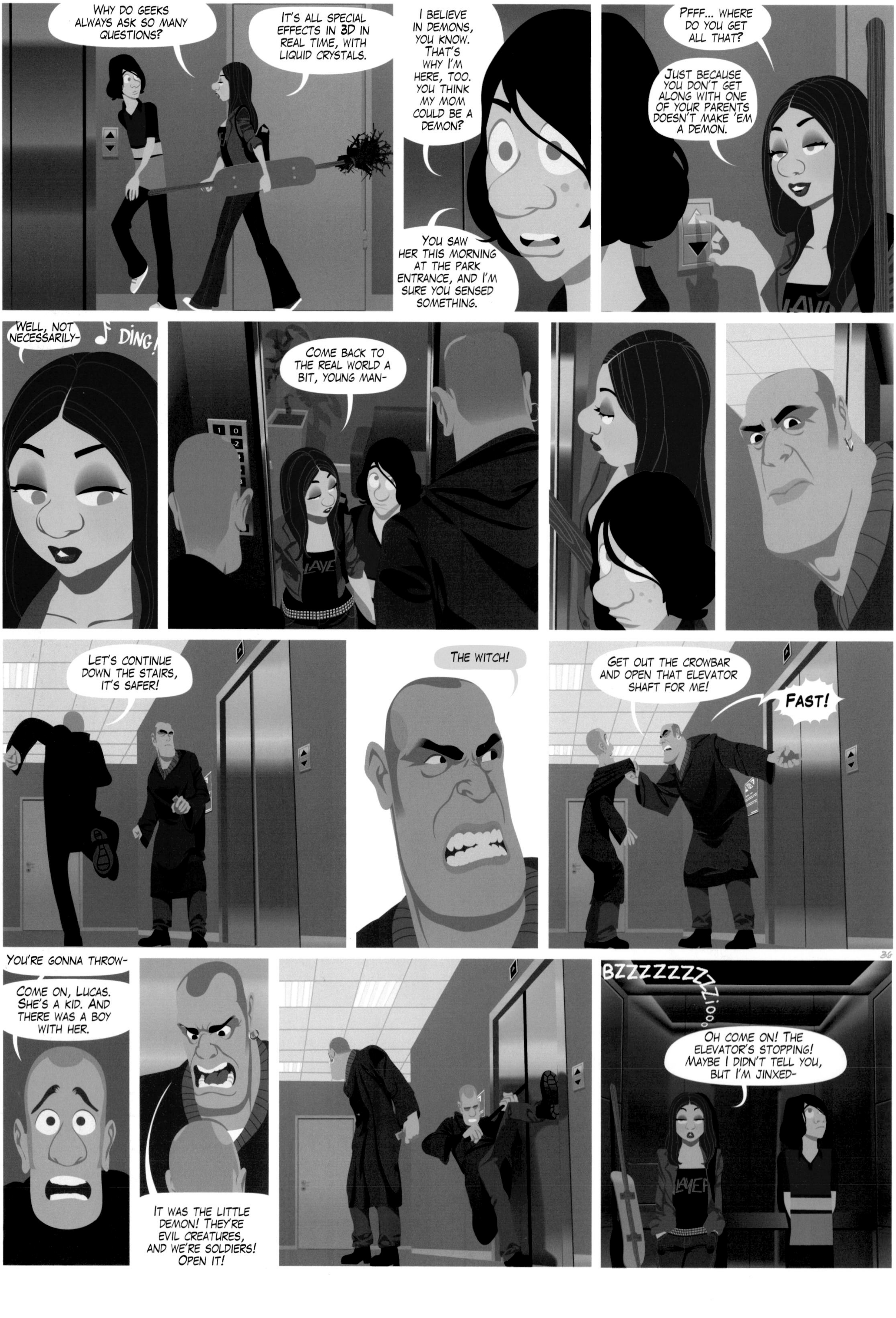
WHY DO GEEKS ALWAYS ASK SO MANY QUESTIONS?
IT'S ALL SPECIAL EFFECTS IN 3D IN REAL TIME, WITH LIQUID CRYSTALS.
I BELIEVE IN DEMONS, YOU KNOW. THAT'S WHY I'M HERE, TOO. YOU THINK MY MOM COULD BE A DEMON?
YOU SAW HER THIS MORNING AT THE PARK ENTRANCE, AND I'M SURE YOU SENSED SOMETHING.
PFFF... WHERE DO YOU GET ALL THAT?
JUST BECAUSE YOU DON'T GET ALONG WITH ONE OF YOUR PARENTS DOESN'T MAKE 'EM A DEMON.
WELL, NOT NECESSARILY-
DING!
COME BACK TO THE REAL WORLD A BIT, YOUNG MAN-
LET'S CONTINUE DOWN THE STAIRS, IT'S SAFER!
THE WITCH!
GET OUT THE CROWBAR AND OPEN THAT ELEVATOR SHAFT FOR ME!
FAST!
YOU'RE GONNA THROW-
COME ON, LUCAS. SHE'S A KID. AND THERE WAS A BOY WITH HER.
IT WAS THE LITTLE DEMON! THEY'RE EVIL CREATURES, AND WE'RE SOLDIERS! OPEN IT!
BZZZZZZZZZiooo
OH COME ON! THE ELEVATOR'S STOPPING! MAYBE I DIDN'T TELL YOU, BUT I'M JINXED-

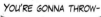

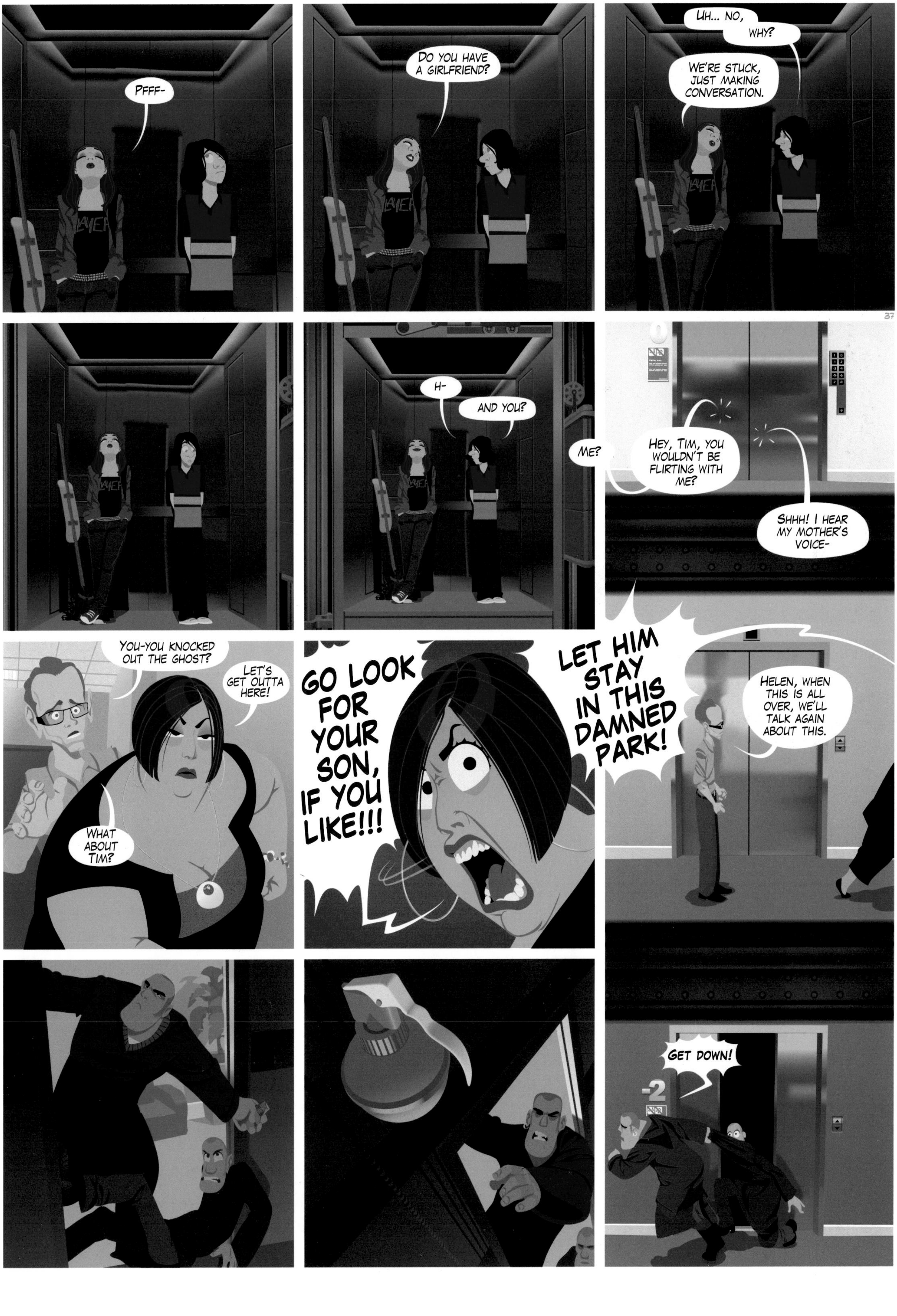
PFFF-
DO YOU HAVE A GIRLFRIEND?
UH... NO,
WHY?
WE'RE STUCK, JUST MAKING CONVERSATION.
H-
AND YOU?
HEY, TIM, YOU WOULDN'T BE FLIRTING WITH ME?
ME?
SHHH! I HEAR MY MOTHER'S VOICE-
YOU-YOU KNOCKED OUT THE GHOST?
LET'S GET OUTTA HERE!
WHAT ABOUT TIM?
GO LOOK FOR YOUR SON, IF YOU LIKE!!!
LET HIM STAY IN THIS DAMNED PARK!
HELEN, WHEN THIS IS ALL OVER, WE'LL TALK AGAIN ABOUT THIS.
-2
GET DOWN!

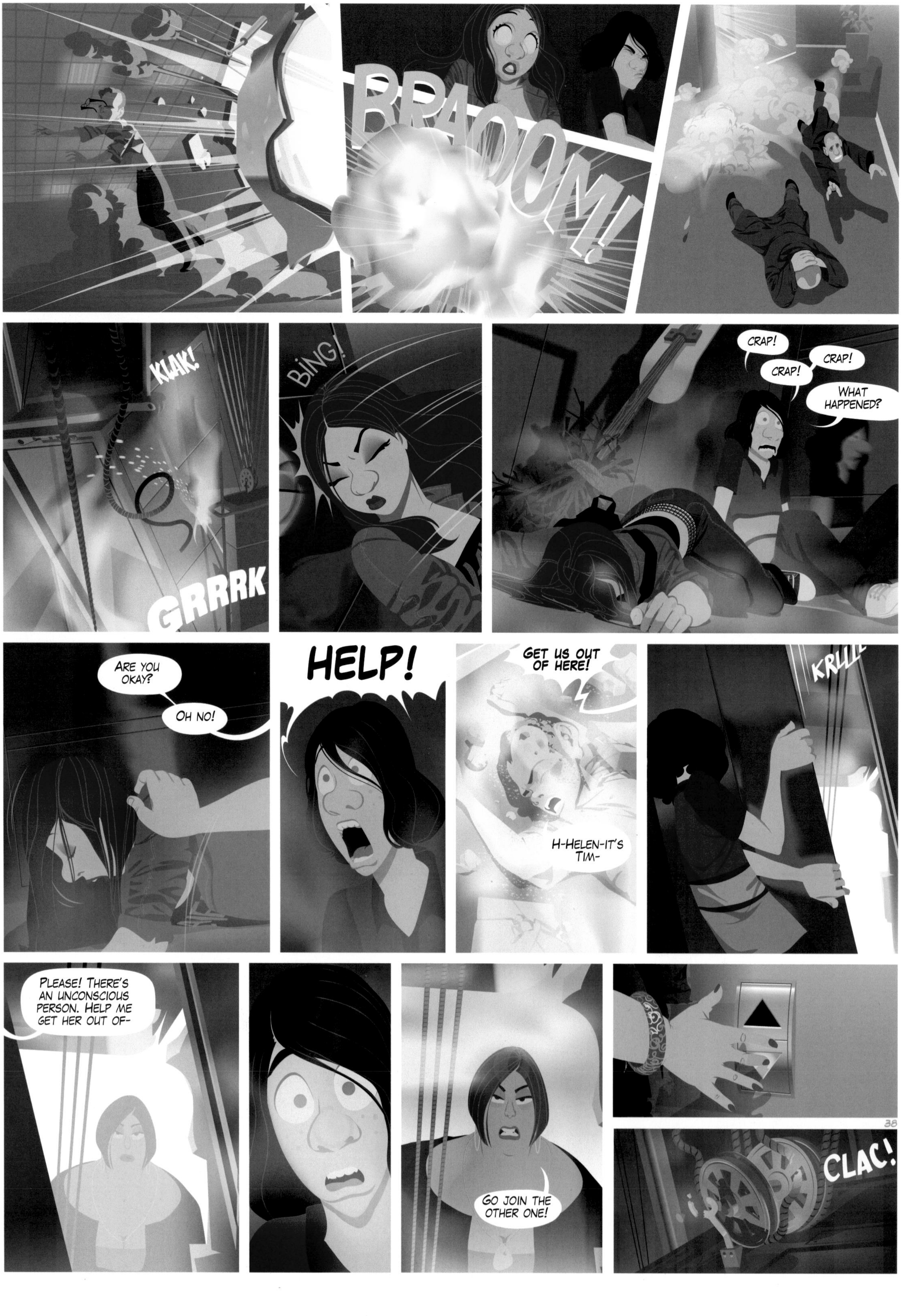
BRAOOM!
KLAK!
GRRRK
BING!
CRAP!
CRAP!
CRAP!
WHAT HAPPENED?
ARE YOU OKAY?
OH NO!
HELP!
GET US OUT OF HERE!
H-HELEN-IT'S TIM-
KRLLL
PLEASE! THERE'S AN UNCONSCIOUS PERSON. HELP ME GET HER OUT OF-
GO JOIN THE OTHER ONE!
CLAC!

CREEEEEEEE
MY SON! DO SOMETHING!

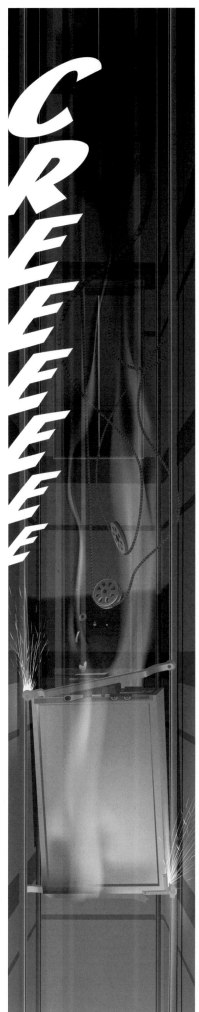

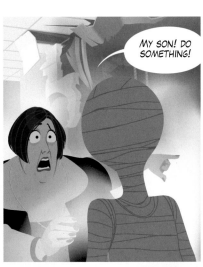

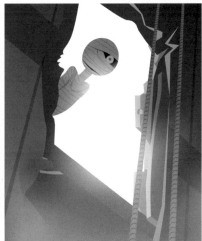

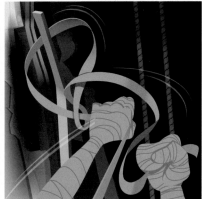

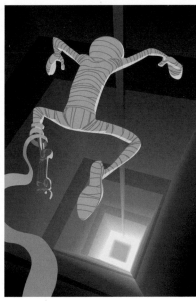

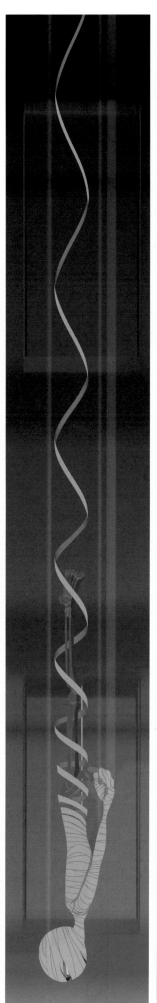

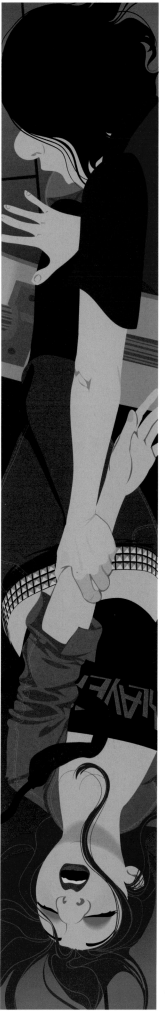

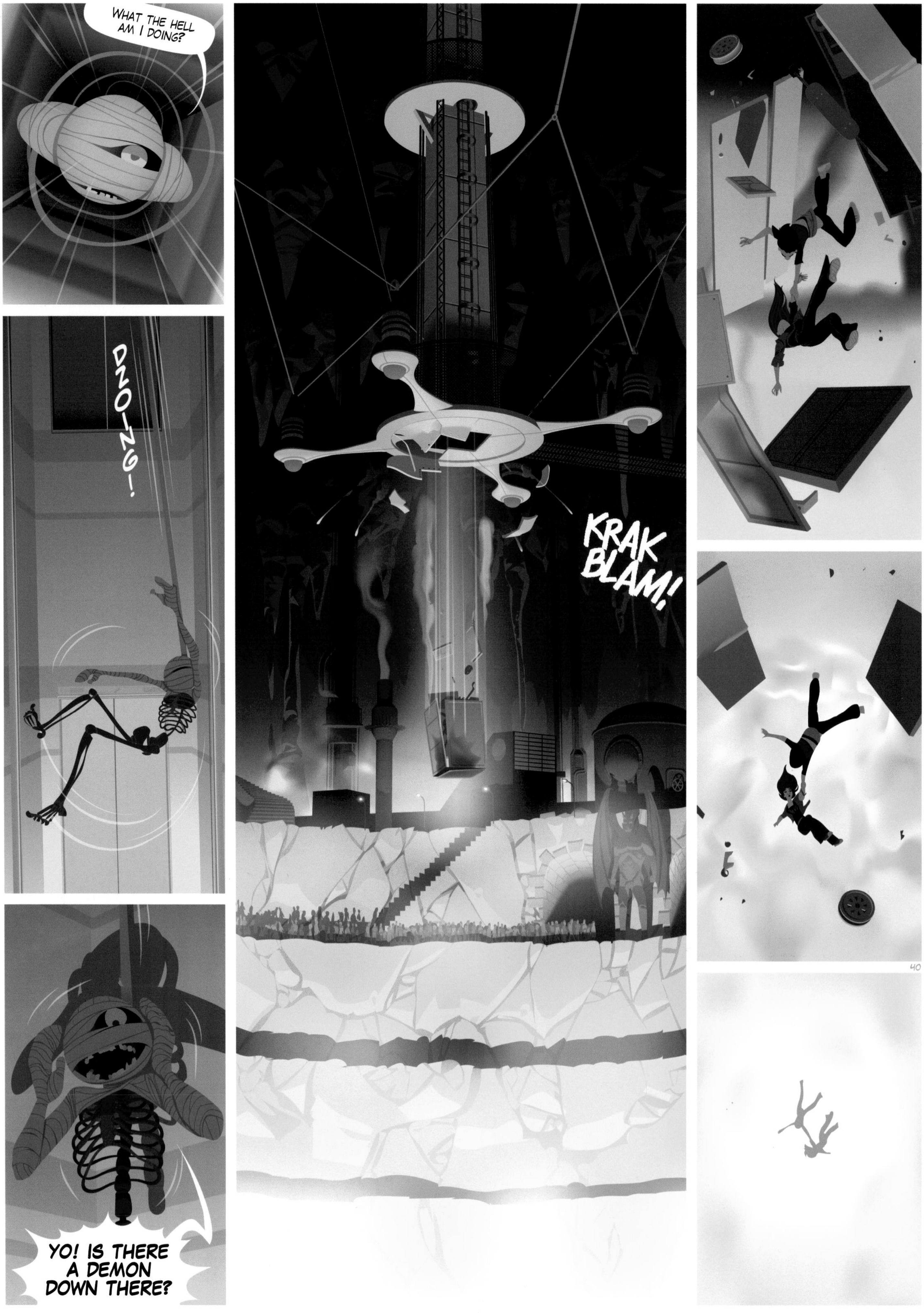
WHAT THE HELL AM I DOING?
DZOING!
YO! IS THERE A DEMON DOWN THERE?
KRAK BLAM!

KLANG!

WHERE THE HELL DID THEY COME FROM? A NEW ATTRACTION?

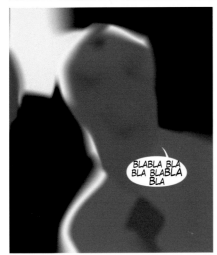
BLABLA BLA BLA BLABLA BLA

AH, SHE'S COMING TO!

WELCOME BACK, LITTLE WITCH!

YOU'RE IN THE INFIRMARY. YOU'RE OKAY.

HOW DO YOU FEEL?

SOMETHING HAPPENED IN THE ELEVATOR, DIDN'T IT?

I LOST TRACK FOR A MOMENT AND I DON'T LIKE THAT.

A GRENADE EXPLODED, AND THE ELEVATOR TOOK A DIZZYING FALL TOWARDS THE FLAMING PIT.

OH.

I HAVE GOOD NEWS AND BAD NEWS-

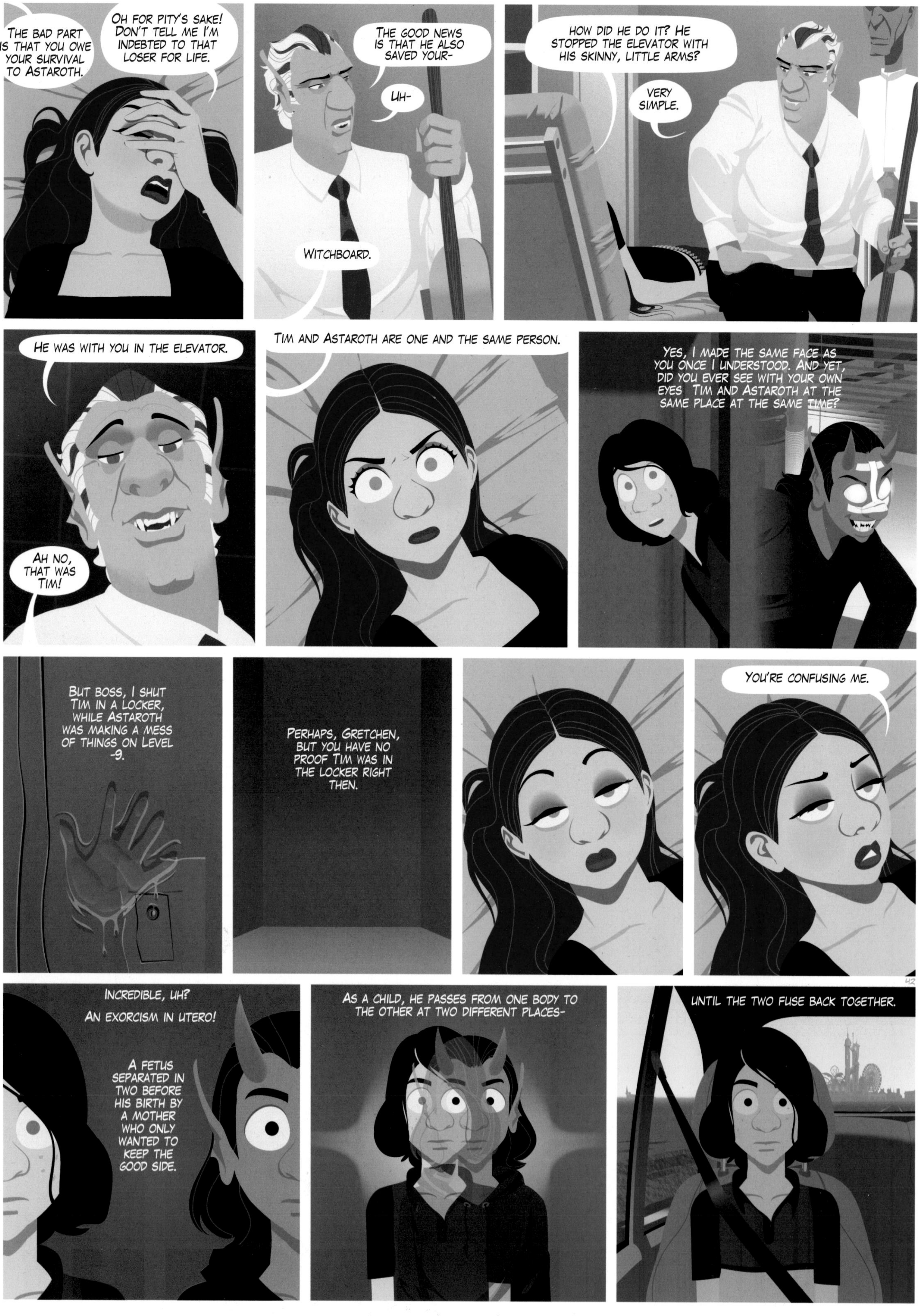

The bad part is that you owe your survival to Astaroth.
Oh for pity's sake! Don't tell me I'm indebted to that loser for life.
The good news is that he also saved your-
Uh-
Witchboard.
How did he do it? He stopped the elevator with his skinny, little arms?
Very simple.
He was with you in the elevator.
Ah no, that was Tim!
Tim and Astaroth are one and the same person.
Yes, I made the same face as you once I understood. And yet, did you ever see with your own eyes Tim and Astaroth at the same place at the same time?
But boss, I shut Tim in a locker, while Astaroth was making a mess of things on Level -9.
Perhaps, Gretchen, but you have no proof Tim was in the locker right then.
You're confusing me.
Incredible, uh?
An exorcism in utero!
A fetus separated in two before his birth by a mother who only wanted to keep the good side.
As a child, he passes from one body to the other at two different places-
Until the two fuse back together.

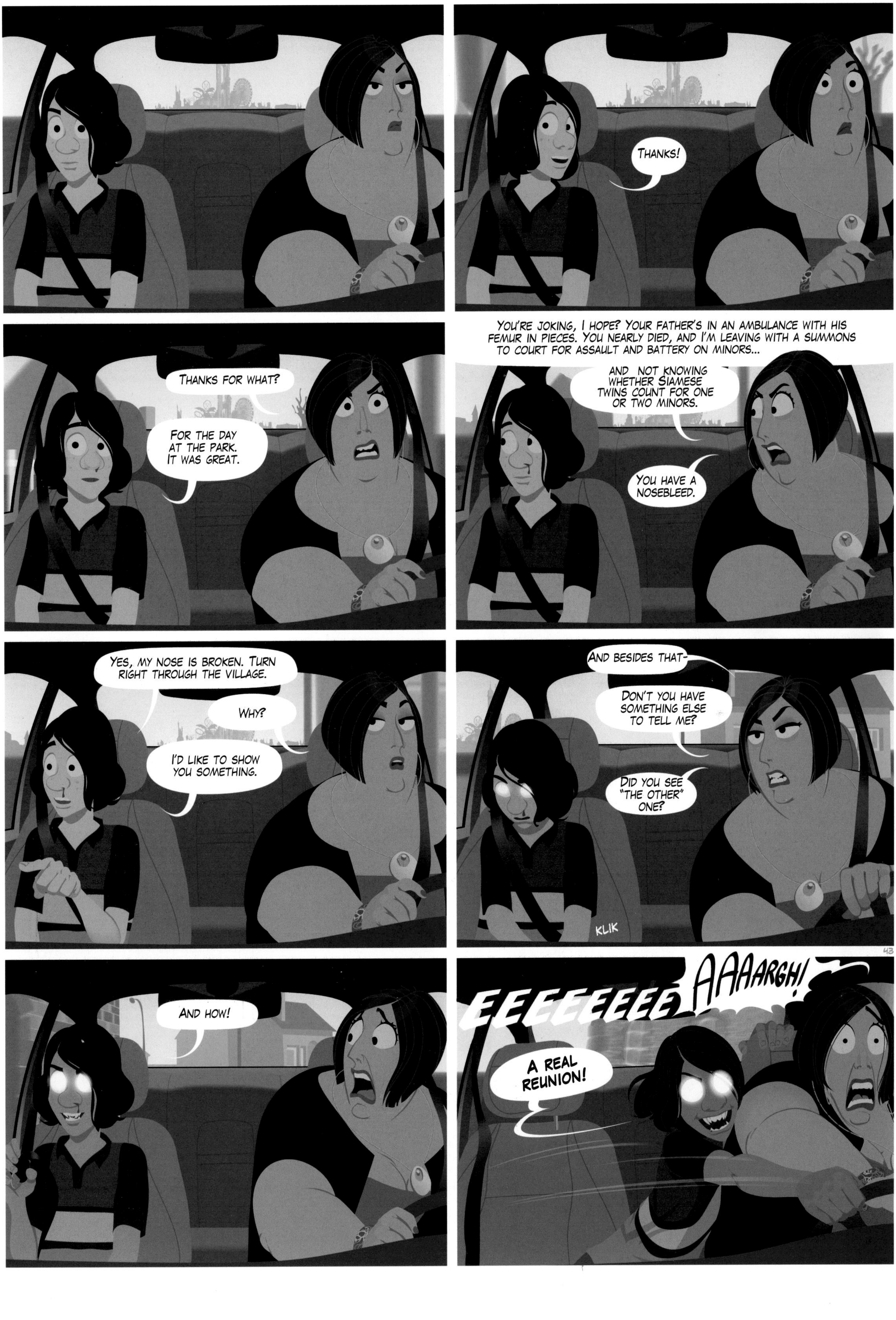
THANKS!
THANKS FOR WHAT?
FOR THE DAY AT THE PARK. IT WAS GREAT.
YOU'RE JOKING, I HOPE? YOUR FATHER'S IN AN AMBULANCE WITH HIS FEMUR IN PIECES. YOU NEARLY DIED, AND I'M LEAVING WITH A SUMMONS TO COURT FOR ASSAULT AND BATTERY ON MINORS...
AND NOT KNOWING WHETHER SIAMESE TWINS COUNT FOR ONE OR TWO MINORS.
YOU HAVE A NOSEBLEED.
YES, MY NOSE IS BROKEN. TURN RIGHT THROUGH THE VILLAGE.
WHY?
I'D LIKE TO SHOW YOU SOMETHING.
AND BESIDES THAT-
DON'T YOU HAVE SOMETHING ELSE TO TELL ME?
DID YOU SEE "THE OTHER" ONE?
KLIK
AND HOW!
EEEEEEEE AAAARGH!
A REAL REUNION!

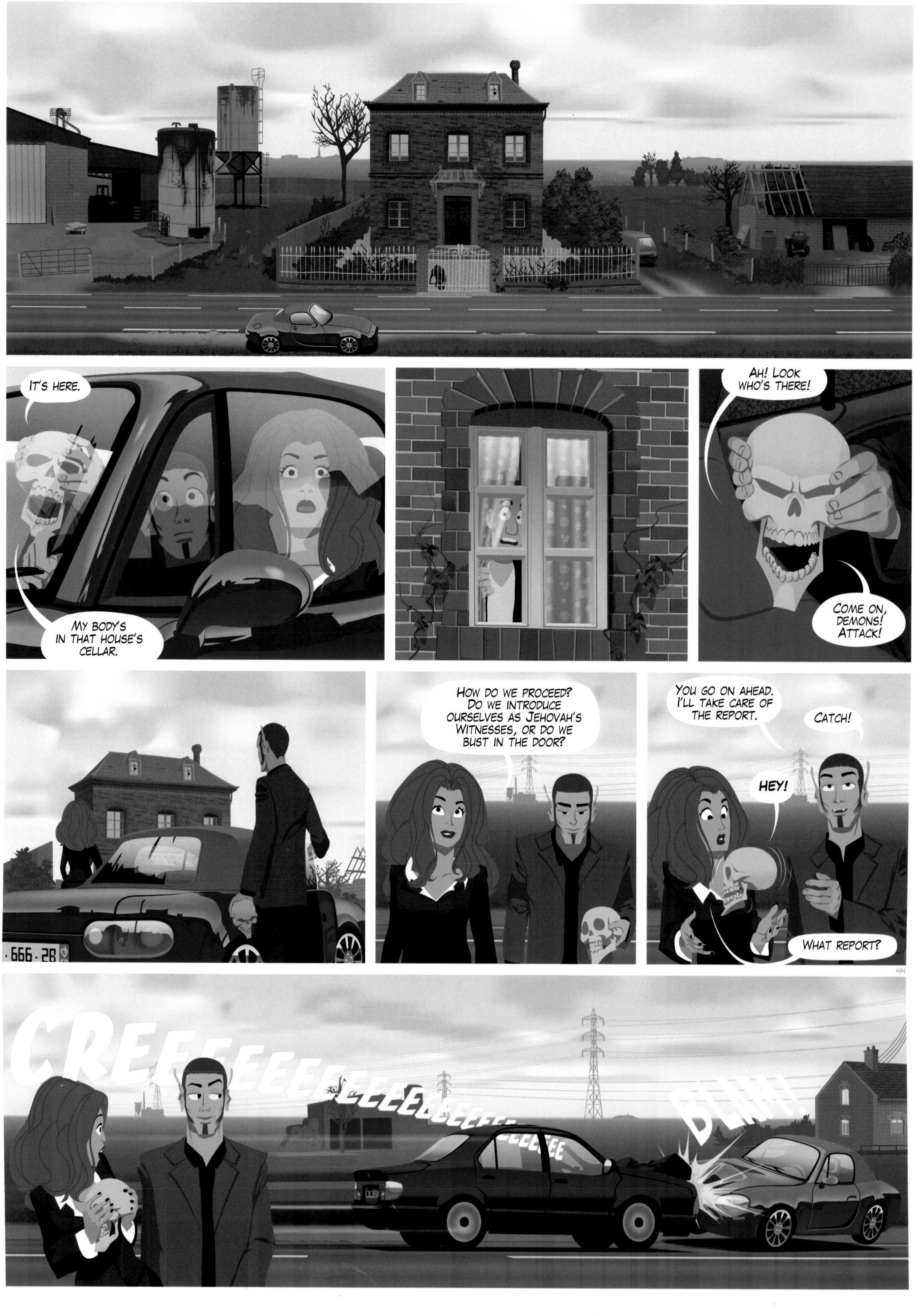
It's here.
My body's in that house's cellar.
Ah! Look who's there!
Come on, demons! Attack!
How do we proceed? Do we introduce ourselves as Jehovah's Witnesses, or do we bust in the door?
You go on ahead. I'll take care of the report.
Catch!
Hey!
What report?
CREEEEEEEEEEEEEEEEEEEEEE
BLAM!

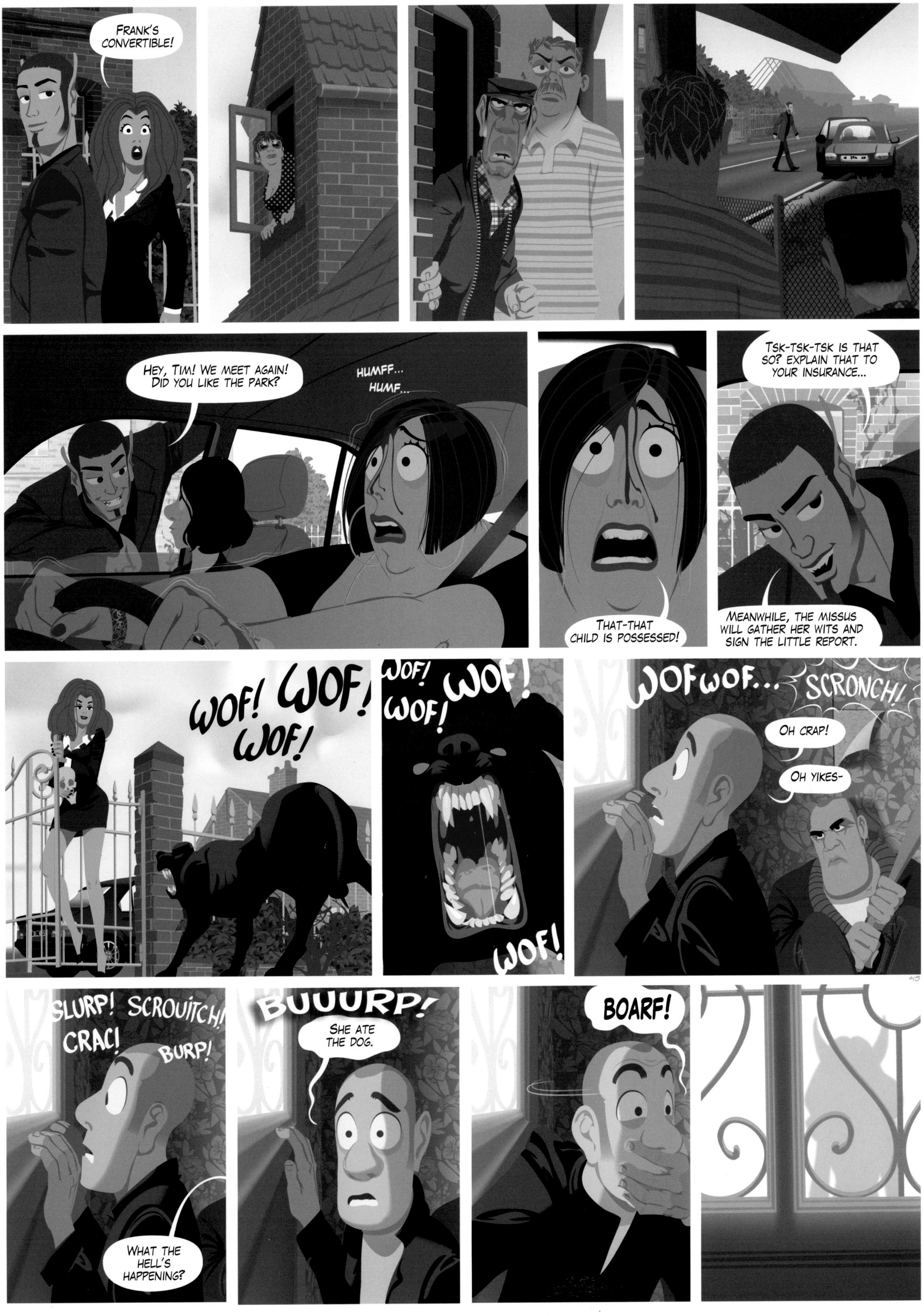
FRANK'S CONVERTIBLE!
HEY, TIM! WE MEET AGAIN! DID YOU LIKE THE PARK?
HUMFF... HUMF...
THAT-THAT CHILD IS POSSESSED!
TSK-TSK-TSK IS THAT SO? EXPLAIN THAT TO YOUR INSURANCE...
MEANWHILE, THE MISSUS WILL GATHER HER WITS AND SIGN THE LITTLE REPORT.
WOF! WOF! WOF!
WOF! WOF! WOF!
WOF!
WOF WOF...
SCRONCH!
OH CRAP!
OH YIKES-
SLURP! SCROUITCH! CRAC! BURP!
WHAT THE HELL'S HAPPENING?
BUUURP!
SHE ATE THE DOG.
BOARF!

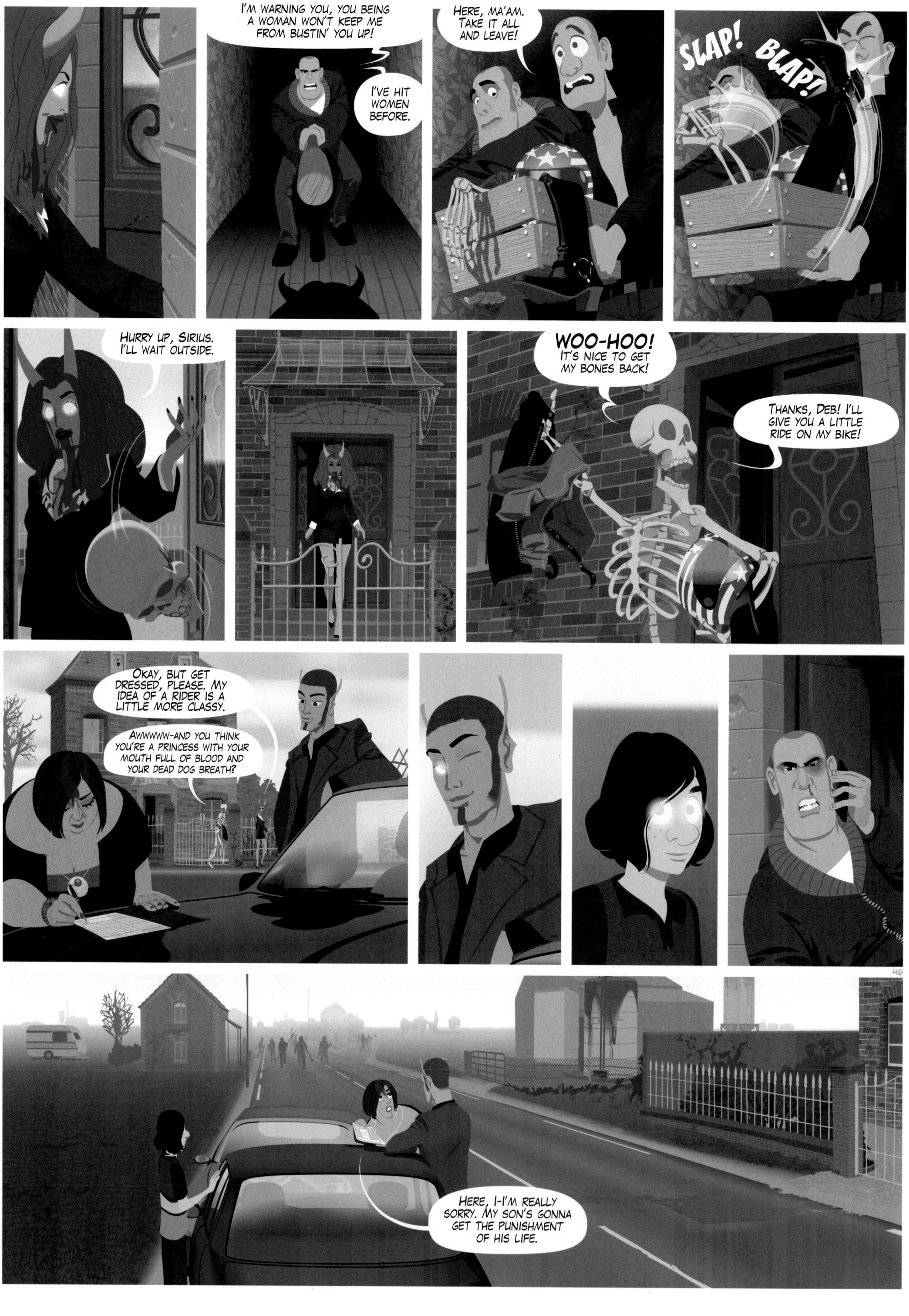
I'M WARNING YOU, YOU BEING A WOMAN WON'T KEEP ME FROM BUSTIN' YOU UP!
I'VE HIT WOMEN BEFORE.
HERE, MA'AM. TAKE IT ALL AND LEAVE!
SLAP! BLAP!
HURRY UP, SIRIUS. I'LL WAIT OUTSIDE.
WOO-HOO! IT'S NICE TO GET MY BONES BACK!
THANKS, DEB! I'LL GIVE YOU A LITTLE RIDE ON MY BIKE!
OKAY, BUT GET DRESSED, PLEASE. MY IDEA OF A RIDER IS A LITTLE MORE CLASSY.
AWWWWW–AND YOU THINK YOU'RE A PRINCESS WITH YOUR MOUTH FULL OF BLOOD AND YOUR DEAD DOG BREATH?
HERE, I-I'M REALLY SORRY. MY SON'S GONNA GET THE PUNISHMENT OF HIS LIFE.

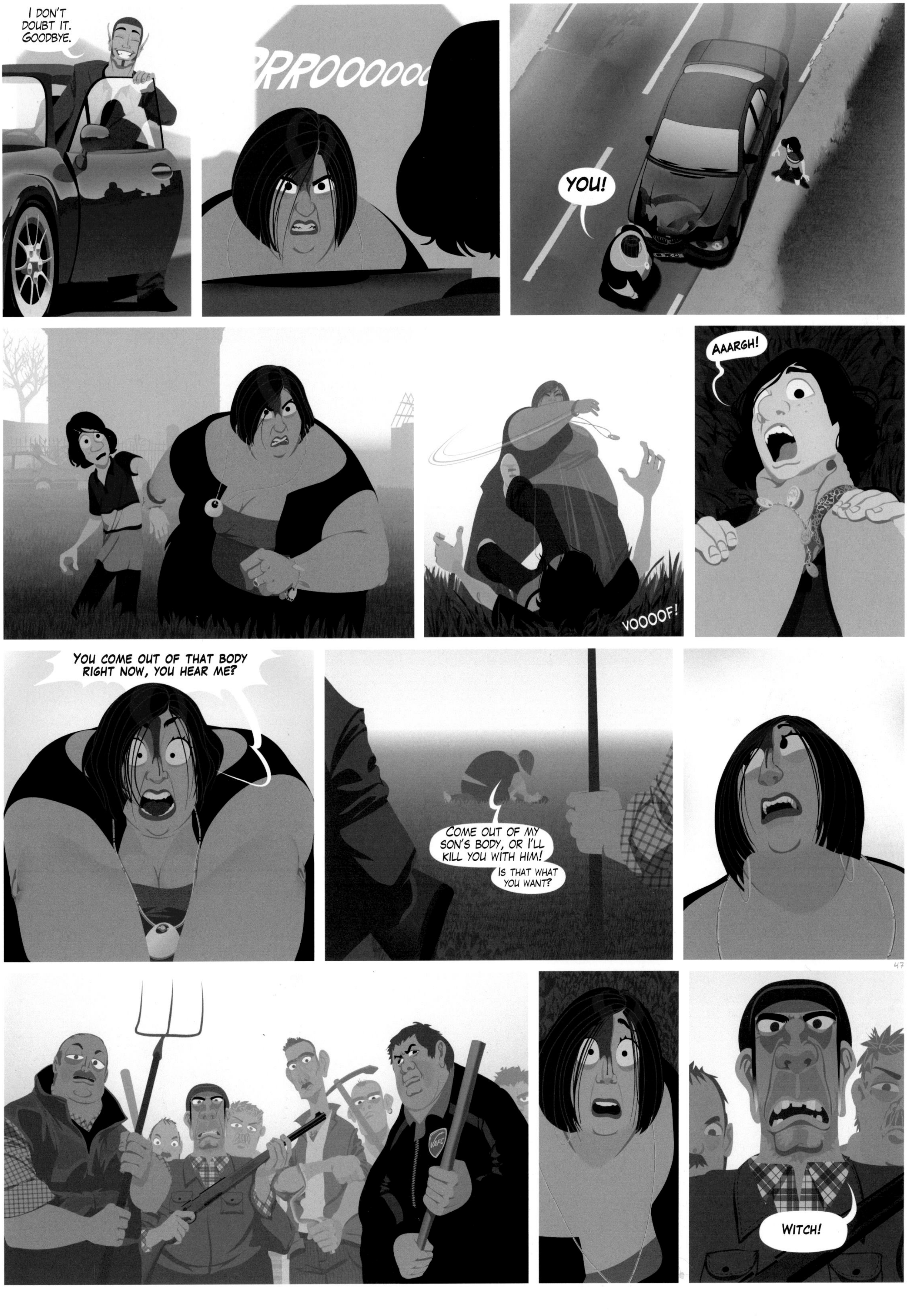

I DON'T DOUBT IT. GOODBYE.
RRROOOOOOO
YOU!
AAARGH!
VOOOOF!
YOU COME OUT OF THAT BODY RIGHT NOW, YOU HEAR ME?
COME OUT OF MY SON'S BODY, OR I'LL KILL YOU WITH HIM!
IS THAT WHAT YOU WANT?
WITCH!

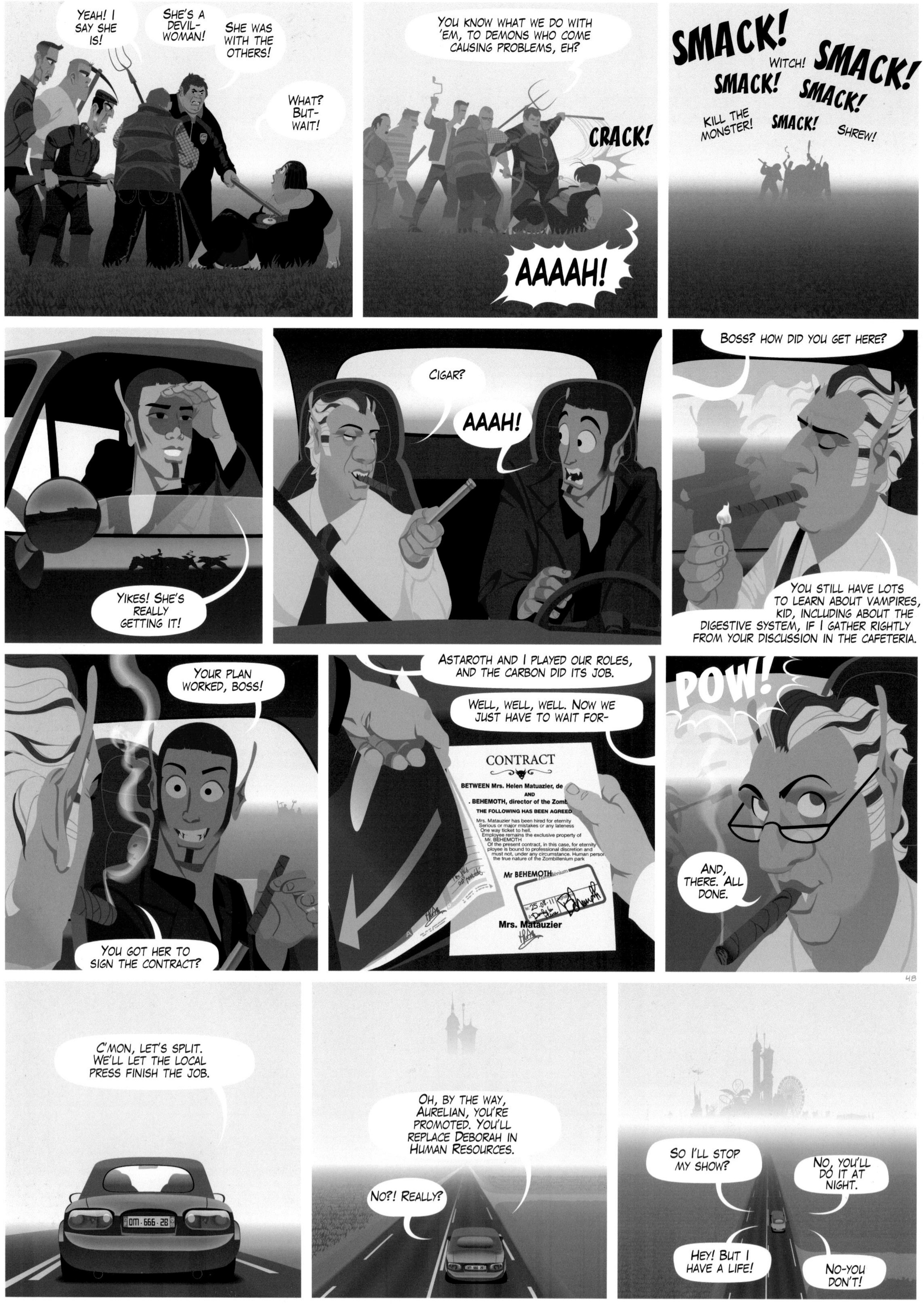
YEAH! I SAY SHE IS!
SHE'S A DEVIL-WOMAN!
SHE WAS WITH THE OTHERS!
WHAT? BUT- WAIT!
YOU KNOW WHAT WE DO WITH 'EM, TO DEMONS WHO COME CAUSING PROBLEMS, EH?
CRACK!
AAAAH!
SMACK!
WITCH!
SMACK!
SMACK!
SMACK!
KILL THE MONSTER!
SMACK!
SHREW!
YIKES! SHE'S REALLY GETTING IT!
CIGAR?
AAAH!
BOSS? HOW DID YOU GET HERE?
YOU STILL HAVE LOTS TO LEARN ABOUT VAMPIRES, KID, INCLUDING ABOUT THE DIGESTIVE SYSTEM, IF I GATHER RIGHTLY FROM YOUR DISCUSSION IN THE CAFETERIA.
YOUR PLAN WORKED, BOSS!
YOU GOT HER TO SIGN THE CONTRACT?
ASTAROTH AND I PLAYED OUR ROLES, AND THE CARBON DID ITS JOB.
WELL, WELL, WELL. NOW WE JUST HAVE TO WAIT FOR-
CONTRACT
BETWEEN Mrs. Helen Matuazier, de
AND
. BEHEMOTH, director of the Zomb
THE FOLLOWING HAS BEEN AGREED
Mrs. Matauzier has been hired for eternity
Serious or major mistakes or any lateness
One way ticket to hell.
Employee remains the exclusive property of
Mr. BEHEMOTH
Of the present contract, in this case, for eternity
ployee is bound to professional discretion and
must not, under any circumstance. Human person
the true nature of the Zombillenium park
Mr BEHEMOTH
Mrs. Matauzier
POW!
AND, THERE. ALL DONE.
C'MON, LET'S SPLIT. WE'LL LET THE LOCAL PRESS FINISH THE JOB.
DM-666-28
OH, BY THE WAY, AURELIAN, YOU'RE PROMOTED. YOU'LL REPLACE DEBORAH IN HUMAN RESOURCES.
NO?! REALLY?
SO I'LL STOP MY SHOW?
NO, YOU'LL DO IT AT NIGHT.
HEY! BUT I HAVE A LIFE!
NO-YOU DON'T!

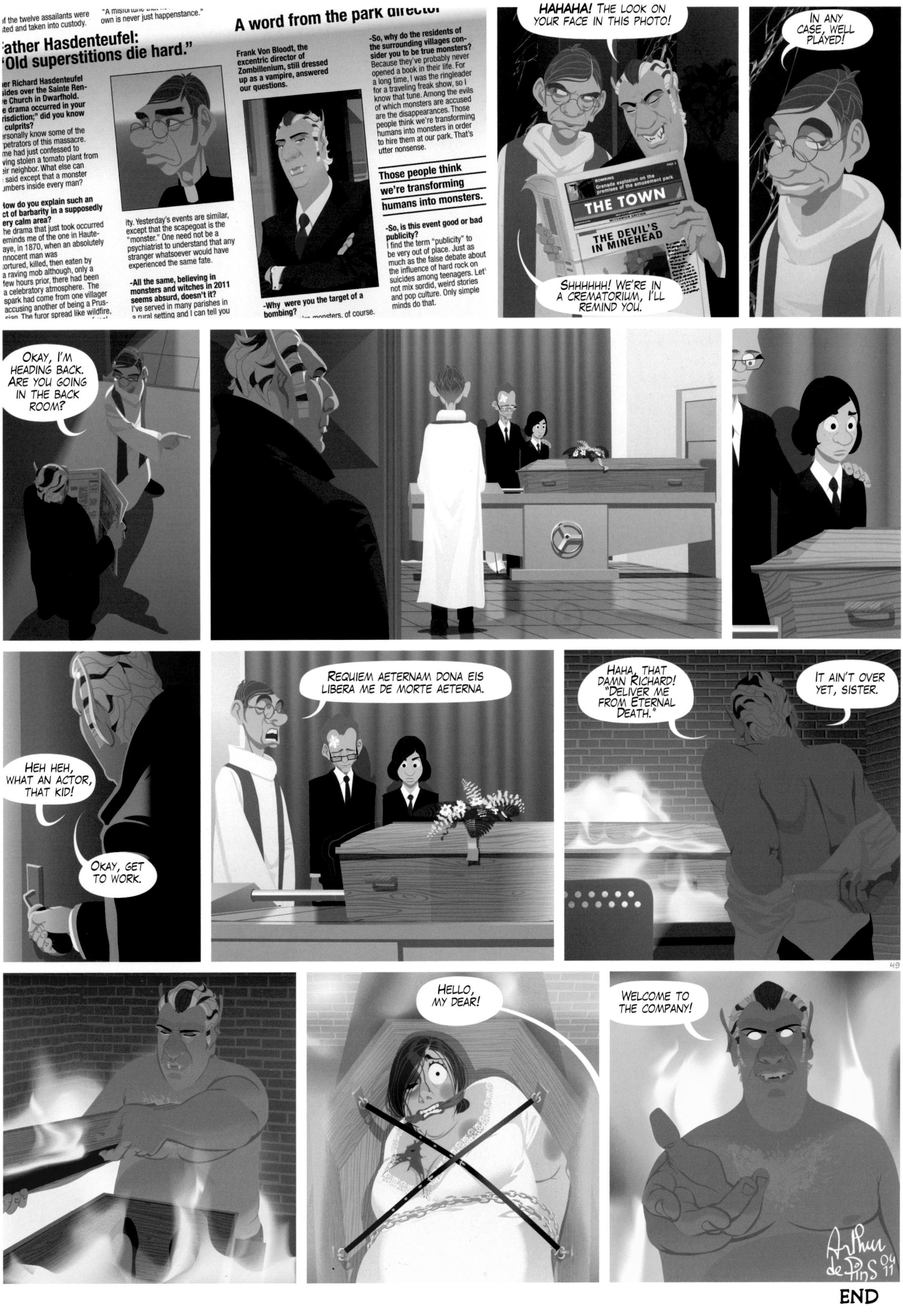

f the twelve assailants were
ted and taken into custody.
own is never just happenstance."
ather Hasdenteufel:
'Old superstitions die hard."
er Richard Hasdenteufel
sides over the Sainte Ren-
e Church in Dwarfhold.
e drama occurred in your
risdiction;" did you know
culprits?
rsonally know some of the
petrators of this massacre.
me had just confessed to
ving stolen a tomato plant from
eir neighbor. What else can
said except that a monster
umbers inside every man?
How do you explain such an
ct of barbarity in a supposedly
ery calm area?
he drama that just took occurred
eminds me of the one in Haute-
aye, in 1870, when an absolutely
nnocent man was
tortured, killed, then eaten by
a raving mob although, only a
few hours prior, there had been
a celebratory atmosphere. The
spark had come from one villager
accusing another of being a Prus-
ity. Yesterday's events are similar, except that the scapegoat is the "monster." One need not be a psychiatrist to understand that any stranger whatsoever would have experienced the same fate.
-All the same, believing in monsters and witches in 2011 seems absurd, doesn't it?
I've served in many parishes in
A word from the park director
Frank Von Bloodt, the excentric director of Zombillenium, still dressed up as a vampire, answered our questions.
-Why were you the target of a bombing?
-So, why do the residents of the surrounding villages consider you to be true monsters?
Because they've probably never opened a book in their life. For a long time, I was the ringleader for a traveling freak show, so I know that tune. Among the evils of which monsters are accused are the disappearances. Those people think we're transforming humans into monsters in order to hire them at our park. That's utter nonsense.
Those people think we're transforming humans into monsters.
-So, is this event good or bad publicity?
I find the term "publicity" to be very out of place. Just as much as the false debate about the influence of hard rock on suicides among teenagers. Let' not mix sordid, weird stories and pop culture. Only simple minds do that.
HAHAHA! THE LOOK ON YOUR FACE IN THIS PHOTO!
THE TOWN
THE DEVIL'S IN MINEHEAD
SHHHHHH! WE'RE IN A CREMATORIUM, I'LL REMIND YOU.
IN ANY CASE, WELL PLAYED!
OKAY, I'M HEADING BACK. ARE YOU GOING IN THE BACK ROOM?
HEH HEH, WHAT AN ACTOR, THAT KID!
OKAY, GET TO WORK.
REQUIEM AETERNAM DONA EIS LIBERA ME DE MORTE AETERNA.
HAHA, THAT DAMN RICHARD! "DELIVER ME FROM ETERNAL DEATH."
IT AIN'T OVER YET, SISTER.
HELLO, MY DEAR!
WELCOME TO THE COMPANY!
Arthur de Pins 04 11

END

Also available:
Zombillenium, vol.1, $14.99
And other spoofs of horror and fantasy:
Boneyard, vols. 1-7
The Dungeon series (multiple volumes)
P&H: add $4 for 1st item, $1 each addt'l

SEE MORE AT NBMPUB.COM
AND ZOMBILLENIUM.COM

We have over 200 titles available
NBM
160 Broadway, Suite 700, East Wing
New York, NY 10038
Catalog available by request
If ordering by mail add $4 P&H 1st item, $1 each addt'l

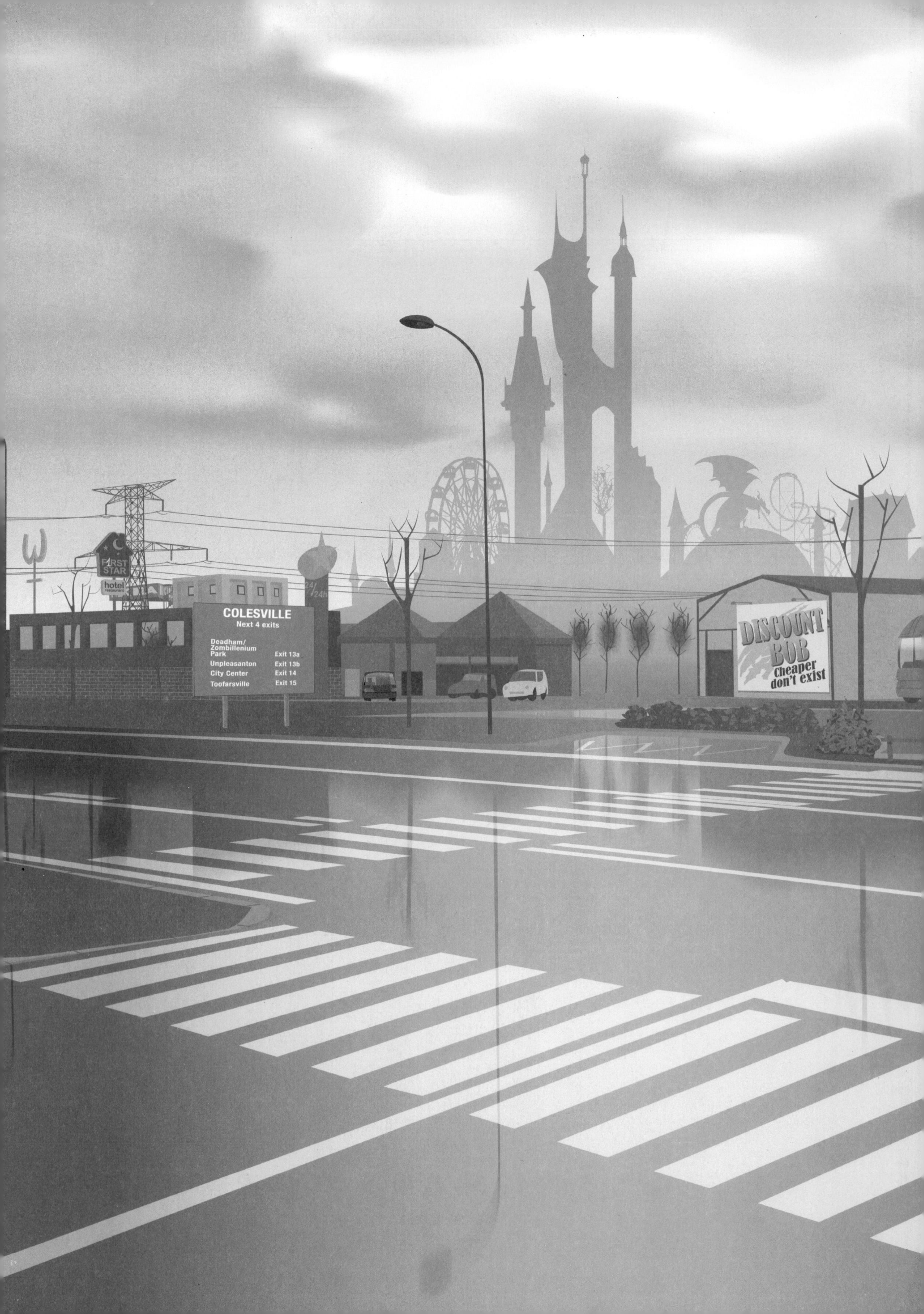
F1RST STAR
hotel
restaurant
24/24h
COLESVILLE
Next 4 exits
Deadham/ Zombillenium Park Exit 13a
Unpleasanton Exit 13b
City Center Exit 14
Toofarsville Exit 15
DISCOUNT BOB
Cheaper don't exist